Printed by CreateSpace.

First Printing, 2014

info@god-thedevil-andi.com

ISBN: 978-0-9930452-3-3

GOD THE DEVIL AND I

BY

JACK JONES

But as for you, man of God, flee these things. Pursue righteousness, godliness, faith, love, endurance and gentleness. - 1 Tim 6:11

One does not become enlightened by imagining figures of light but by making the darkness conscious. - Carl Jung

The desire to reveal is greater than the desire to conceal. - Carl Jung

This page is intentionally left blank.

DEDICATION

I would like to dedicate this book to Alison Hurst. My saviour, ally, best friend, advocate and confidant. A serendipitous Angelic figure. Matriarchal and surrogate Mother to the multitudes. She has selflessly rescued me as a lone stranger, fed, ministered, prayed, and supported diligently for many years. Has offered her home as a refuge and healing place. Gone to extremes along my journey, by my side. Defender and protector. Kept safe and secure. Loyally devoted, committed and steadfast to the end. Has made innumerable personal sacrifices and denied herself that I may receive comfort and solace. Adopted as an orphan and integrated into her family as one of them. Has wept, endured numerous sleepless nights and shared my pain, without provocation or exhortation. Stood, side by side through every crevice, valley, adversity, trial and personal suffering. A rock of salvation. The first person to acknowledge, pronounce and proclaim the accolade, “A remarkable man”, and “A rare gift from God”.

The selfless ministry received from Alison wouldn’t have been possible had it not been for an incredible Godly man, her husband, Alan. The trust bequeathed, selfless attitude and pastoral traits. An advocate opposed to antagonist. To promote and empower. Pursue good over evil and Love over Sin. I would like to credit Alan for being a mutual saviour in my life. His role and responsibility un-quantifiable. To edify and promote another man to restoration, healing and redemption via one’s own wife is inconceivable and incredulous in modern times.

Without this miraculous, unprecedented, supernatural love and affection, not only would the book have not been written, but I wouldn’t be here to write it.

Contents

PREFACE

A harbinger and catalyst for commissioning the God The Devil And I book, was the deeply profound life changing experience of Jack Jones. An epic extraordinarily incomprehensible journey.

Inspired by one young boy's journey from birth, exemplary fortitude and life alchemy experiences. Originating from South Yorkshire, England. A test of survival in the midst of opposition, enemies, detractors and antagonists. Unknown and unseen by every living phenomenon. Called by God to be a warrior to fight beasts and evil forces.

Topics addressed include child development, poverty, poor schooling, social issues, relationships, trauma, dysfunctional families, roles, identities, and wider society. Abuse and mental health issues.

Uncontrived or fabricated but based on a "Calling". A true story. Called to bring light into a dark world. Justice to the unjustified. Expose the failings of the "Establishment". Liberate and instil confidence in those around the world that are the silent suffragettes. Set the captives free, held in bondage and prisoners in their own lives. Bringing hope to the lost. Faith to the faithless. Support victims of trauma, abuse and neglect. By the medium of my own life experience.

Educate, inform and promote the reality of mental health. Psychology, spirituality, philosophy, character, endurance, fortitude and diligence. Dispel the myths and legends that the general population have adopted as standard. The human spirit and the enduring ability of the soul to survive. A Philanthropic endeavour.

Introduction

The first chapter begins in "The Room". The period is year 2007. Jack is now thirty six years old. The subsequent epiphany and revelation will be divulged in Volume Two, the second book. Seemingly contradictory, the book begins towards the end of Jack's journey. Chapter Two presents the beginning in terms of birth, formative years, and early childhood. The foundation, geographic location, family, and environment. Sequential and consecutive chapters chronicle the progressive scenes and events as the months and years prevail.

THE ROOM

It's been five long loathsome years; nearly six. Marvelling at the fractal clouds; as I lay on my bed, hoping for an enigma, a reason why, meaning and purpose. Synonymous with the eponymous Robinson Crusoe; as the ocean ebbs and flows and as an old grandfather clock's pendulum swings to and fro; time eludes me. Pondering, pontificating, perplexed and paranoid. Etching and sketching the tally chart of time. We who tally time by marks in sand or on a wall are proof ourselves that without mark or hope we are but a seamless sentence.

Pardoned, you think of this as some failed guillotine. I, awaiting rescue always meander beach to beach in hope of finding not the bare footprint of the unsought indigenous but any trace of invasion shod. Incubated, marooned and cocooned in this desolate place; the room. These marks were neither in sand nor wall but the deep recesses of consciousness; indelibly inset. When loneliness and isolation exceeds the normal parameters of humanity; one knows instinctively and inherently the cumulative increment of time. The soul has its own clock and recording mechanisms.

Genesis

Gen 1:27
So God created man and woman in his own image. God looked at what he had made and was very pleased.

Sheffield, reside within the county of South Yorkshire, along with the neighbouring towns of Barnsley, Rotherham, and Doncaster. The region was synonymous with the likes of the North East and South Wales. In that the steel production and mining became the fabric and mainstay of community and society alike. These were working-class regions. Parochially, men were men. And well, women were women. The stereotypical man adorned a broadly austere, stoic, stony disposition. Uncompromising, unashamed, unyielding, abrasive. Opaque at best. On the receiving end you may be condescendingly berated. Hard-working, particularly physical, manual, menial work. Inherent by their virtue of their forefathers and predecessors, behaviour, attitudes, social nuances, roles and habits defined. Language broad and common, even digressing into their own hybrid languages, contrived from slang, poor education, socially deprived communities and mutually bad habits from their peers. This hard-working "bread winner", assumed the position of head of the home all its norms, duties, ceremonies, and routines. Making the decisions, managing the finances, planning social/leisure time, through self-determination. Also, the grocery list and weekly staples dictated. A cultural norm; his evening meal—'tea', as they say in Yorkshire—must be waiting on the table, ready to go, on his return from work. Women generally known as 'house wives or home makers'. Bound to the making of a home, cleaning, cooking, shopping, and mothering any children. Education wasn't a forethought or a career or even a lowly job. Obvious exceptions ...if a young lady had gone to Grammar School or was fortunate enough to attend university, she might become a professional person in status and class. Maybe a doctor, banker, accountant, or solicitor.

The family home situated to the north of the city, a small historic village dating back to the fifteenth century adjacent to what was once one of Europe's largest council housing estates, the Manor. A new private housing estate was built in 1968 juxtaposed to these two locations. In that plot, Jack's parents bought their first home. They would bear three children. Jack, Josh, and Paul. Paul was born first in '68, Josh three years later, and Jack thirty-minutes thereafter. Twins. His parents were descendant's of broken families, absent fathers and mothers whom were incapable of being parents. The Manor a forlorn dystopian sprawling metropolis of homogeneous grey houses, tersely worded signs, litter strewn, impoverished, and unkempt. A spirit of melancholy would make its home there.

Jack was born a very special boy. Prolific, precocious, and cognisant. Who would surpass expectation and excel. Become something he wasn't. A metamorphosis by decree of the Most High. Possessing an inscrutable disposition. Achieve anything he turned his hand to. The world really was his oyster. Complemented by his bleached Scandinavian blonde hair and gorgeous blue eyes, meek, mild, inherently passive with a pacifist persona. Unwittingly gifted, gentle, humble soul. Ignorant of his traits. A naturally forgiving, merciful nature, missing exhortation, or chastisement. Despite the aforementioned, excruciatingly shy, reserved, and hidden. On the rare occasion daring to reveal a portion, raw beauty would emerge. Cheeky, enamoured with humour. Notwithstanding sweet and innocent. However, an unlawful impediment would permeate his being, unbeknown. Lying dormant, but effective. The enemy within. Jack had an irrevocable supernatural calling on his life. God had called him from the beginning. A very strong calling. Called by name ... Jack, you are called. An antithesis of self, a dichotomous soul, and warring factions would resonate. The powers of heaven and hell were at their command posts. Angels and demons.

For we wrestle not against flesh and blood, but against principalities, against powers, against the rulers of the darkness of this world, against spiritual wickedness in high places. (Ephesians 6:12 KJV)

A defining moment known as "The Great Endurance".

For I am persuaded, that neither death, nor life, nor angels, nor principalities, nor powers, nor things present, nor things to come, Nor height, nor depth, nor any other creature, shall be able to separate us from the love of God, which is in Christ Jesus our Lord. (Romans 8:38-39 KJV)

But also a curse. To condemn, disparage, distort and destroy. A thief in the night. Incognito, with legions of ranks, warriors, foot soldiers, generals and infantry men.

The thief comes only to steal, kill, and destroy; I have come that they may have life, and in abundance. (John 10:10 NIV)

Nil By Mouth

I will not leave you as orphans; but will come to you. John 14:18

My sixth sense alerted different. No one was ever going to tell me. They couldn't enter my world. A sense of ultimate and definite, wholly complete irrefutable alienation. Signs, quirks, and oddities also brought me to this conclusion. Left outside of our house during the day at an age considered neglect. A feeling of dis-connection, unbound, isolation, aloof around 'appropriate adults'. Banging my head on the floor with absolute 'full blown' indignant rage in the midst of 'Family'. Merciless of pain inflicted. The overwhelming compulsion eclipsed any feeble attempt to refrain or restrain. An inability to speak. Boys and girls on the street arriving at my face, holding a single finger up, and bursting into rapturous hysterical laughter. Unable to suppress the awkward sensation. A period of great entertainment for the contemporary participants, who would dutifully recite this daily ritual, for another 'Laugh'. Scant friends. Always going to be difficult, unspoken. The kids known were casual acquaintances. In which case associated with a mutual connection. An intrinsic, poor self image would abide. Inherently jealous and envious. Arrogant, only in the way of a superiority complex over-shadowing a well rooted inferiority complex. Confounded from the beginning. Devoid of emotion. Abject terror, fear, anxiety and worry my friends.

Nursery, a strange experience. Mother would drop me off. Enraged; feeling total abandonment. Kicking, screaming, yelling, and crying for my life. Believing discarded, never to be re-united. Failing to ever re-engage. A very 'clingy' child, with Josh but also with Mother. The nursery children would relate and play together in unison. Again, knowingly incongruous. Unattached to anyone, the children or nursery staff. Aloof, ostracised by default. Them and me. Missing us. Unspoken and they won't speak to me. Alienation sets in. But knowing I'm different.

Deemed appropriate now fit to walk ourselves to school. Five years old. Apparently, looking after each other. My intuition knew; premature, denied, neglected and expected to be older than our years.

We used to sit together in class. Josh was much more socially confident and advanced in comparison. We were like chalk-and-cheese, poles apart. Outwardly self-assured as opposed to my inward introspective demeanour. Able to effortlessly make friends and enter conversation uninvited. Comfortable approaching teachers, pupils or strangers, circumventing fear and self-doubt. I'd be too afraid to ask the teacher to go to the toilet. A request to Josh, on my behalf; and would duly comply. Then the intrepid journey across the classroom; down the corridor; into the toilets and back again. Hoping an invisible human-being would cross my path en-route. My body almost skimming and gliding along the walls bracing myself. Like an animal instinct; avoiding any potential predator. If such a scenario should present itself my body freezing, in fear and terror. Cowering as a distressed runt exposed to its finality. Once the moment had passed regaining my composure and continuing this terrifying experience of going to the toilet alone. They soon clocked on what was happening. How my whole dependence on Josh was restricting both our development. Decided without consultation we'd be split-up. My greatest fear. If I wasn't traumatised enough, defunct and failing; immediate vital support was paramount. On my own. A runt exposed to all the creatures in the jungle.

An ambivalence towards teachers. We had two. One abrasive, corrosive, abrupt, and cutting. The other gentle, calm, and warm. My innate instincts automatically drew me to the more secure, safe, reliable teacher. And consequently would avoid

Mrs Davis at all cost. Lambasted for being late; not of my own accord incidentally. Scarred for life. On another occasion; forgetting my P.E kit resulting in having to do it in pants. Another great humiliation. So vulnerable, ashamed, and exposed. A great indignity; helpless to change. My inherent self awareness alerted again I was peculiar. All the other children would accomplish the task of 'Expression'. Jumping, leaping, raised arms, running, ultimate free uninhibited display. Not me. Bound. Hands pinned to hips. Frozen in fear. Any attempt to participate render overwhelmed; accosted by fear. Days became filled with horror, terror, and acute fear as a matter of course. Every scenario met with trepidation and reticence. During assembly requiring the toilet. But couldn't bring myself to interrupt proceedings. The fear of pest, nuisance or burden. Eventually the inevitable happened. Wetting myself. Sitting in the puddle on the wood laminate floor. Compounding an already brewing low self-esteem.

We were once found playing on the school field while the tractor cut the grass. A group of us caught and summoned to sit outside the headmasters' office. The word got around, seriously in trouble. What a loathsome, heinous crime we had committed. Again in assembly found crying. The children in front turned around enquiring of my distress. Like life and death. They were going to kill me as punishment. Completely irrational but believable. Slowly but surely the notion derived that every human-being is a potential predator. Mistrustful of all. Going through this routine, mute; controlled by abject terror. Days became lonely. But knowing the alienation. Exceptionally long days. Incapacitated to discern I was different. Submitting rhetorical statements or platitudes.

"That's how he is, shy. He doesn't speak."
They had accepted a hidden child.

Obvious at this stage: an intrinsic ability had adjoined to my soul, to repress, subdue and override the tumult within but also external environmental challenges. Wilfully opting to deny, rebuke and refute. In denial. An inherent, self-sustainability, preservation, and human trait to survive. Imbued to cope, instil peace and self reassurance. These inbuilt innate strategies were part of my creation. Who I was. Shove every sensation, feeling, and experience deep down. Self numbing. A counter reaction to despairing, anxiety-ridden, and traumatised.

Mother was a part-time dinner lady at another school. She took me with her on this particular day. Too ill to go to school and she had to work therefore taken along. Again, a terrifying experience surrounded by dinner ladies. The school kitchen environment; an alien experience. The mêlée and frenetic activity typical of a school kitchen at lunchtime. Strikingly poignant; my seat the complete poles opposite of the table; next to someone unfamiliar. Staring at Mother; for all intents and purposes she might have been just another dinner lady. Devastated internally. The penny dropped. Unconnected at all. Doesn't get how I tick or feel. Might as well be one of the many unknown to me. The immediate sensations were: remorseful, sorrowful, disenfranchised, tearful and sad, missing vocal expression.

Oddly, waking up one Sunday morning; walking down stairs; opening the kitchen door fully expectant to be greeted and asked what I would like for breakfast. Zilch. A vacuum of acknowledgement. Assuming the position; duly looked after myself. Often the case.

We were learning to swim at the time. Possessing arm-bands and the proverbial 1970's polystyrene float. Mum and Dad would sit in the balcony and watch as taught by an instructor. However, on this occasion different. On arrival at the pool, a babies' pen, invariably full of arm-bands. Empty. By the time I had made the approach and conducted a full assessment of the situation, the conclusion a resounding "Shit!". Anxieties kicked in at full speed. Unthinkable to ask anyone. A Nuisance or burden. I'll just go in. Josh already well in, buoyant with both arm-bands intact. This particular pool had those graduating steps. Whereby enter ankle-deep and increasingly penetrate further depth as you proceed. Seconds before the high-water mark of my body height 3ft, was reached. That was it. Lost my footing. I'm in. Literally. Well in; far too deep. Too late to turn back. I'm on my way. "Shit!". The realisation sets in; I've made a humongous blunder. Drifting aimlessly; flapping; panicking, going under towards Josh. Reassuring at first thought. He would save me. I could see; in the mêlée, kerfuffle, panic, trauma, and blurred vision. He could see me, safe with arm-bands well buoyant. The next moment would escalate and exacerbate an already precarious situation to one of incredulity. On submersion my body would naturally re-emerge. But on the ascent would force my head back under. The process repeating for what felt like minutes. Then I was going … unconscious. Next thing on the side of the pool resuscitated; wearing an oxygen mask.

As well as left to our own devices; walking ourselves to school, the responsibility for punctuality, remembering what to take to school. Now deemed appropriate, we could take ourselves to the local barbers. All too much. Socially defunct and inept. At seven years old conversing, connecting, and conforming to adult norms; an unknown phenomenon. Starting point mute. Josh wouldn't go anywhere with me. Great contempt, disdain, and resentment from the beginning. Despised me. My response: redundant and non-reactionary. Innocent, confused and perplexed at this incongruous behaviour. Although attached to great sadness, disappointment and loss. Sensing an god-given phenomenon of mutually exclusive twins, being severed, dismembered and separated before my very eyes. Unable to alter, modify or fix. Aware my co-joined, inextricably linked other-half is denying me. My anxieties compounded and failing. I tried. On this occasion, the lady at the barbers would comment:
"Take a look at this!" to her colleague.

A bald patch on my scalp. It turned out to be alopecia; an anxiety disorder. The doctor prescribed ointment. Circumventing the rigour of medical exploration, enquiry, or diagnosis to elucidate root cause. They also thought it a good idea to send us dancing. Yes, you heard it right the first time! Bloody dancing. Again, we'd make our own way there and back unattended. Sent as instructed and encouraged but not of our own volition. Also exhorted to join the Boys Brigade, Josh and I; just down the road. Again, take ourselves off, deal with the social situation, unattended and unsupported. Arriving anxious with trepidation unknowing of what might unfold; unattended prior. Hovering around failing to connect or engage. Standing aloof, waiting for someone to lead, welcome, induct or at least be hospitable.

The weekly ritual was to visit Dad's mother, the other Nan. He worked six days Monday to Saturday; Sunday was the Sabbath, day of rest. He would go to the pub with his step-dad and we'd be left with Nan until his return. A park lay within fifty yards of Nan's house. A big park with a pond for boats, ducks, and fishing. Paul would be ten so deemed fit we could go fishing together and would somehow look after me. Unaware how to tackle up, thread the line through the eyes, put the float on or even tie a hook. Absent of instruction or explanation. Somehow the rod, line, float, and hook would meet. Albeit precariously, cobbled together on a trial-and-error basis. God help me if the float ever went under and a fish had managed to consume the maggot ultimately hooking itself. Continually going to Paul, enquiring to cast and hook the bait. What shall I do if it goes under? But telling at this age. Rejected, dismissed, spurned, told to sit there and watch the float. Compliant for three straight hours. Unflinching; took my eye off the ball, looked left nor right. But stared intently at this immutable float. Transfixed in a trance. The conditioning of rebuttal, rebuke and refute had already made its mark. The learning commendable. I had got it. Don't approach anyone for help or assistance. Do everything on your own ability and limited understanding. Do you want to be reminded of how painful it is; unworthy of time and attention? Insignificant, undeserving of effort. Prevent and preserve. Avoid the degrading humiliation for your own self preservation. Don't go there. Figure out all the unknowns, problems and difficulties yourself. Without instruction, tutoring, mentoring, pastoring, or patriarchal paternal input.

We had a rabbit, the other two would look after it. Feed and clean, when they remembered, hold and try and catch it when it escaped out of the hutch. Passing it to me to hold but would freak-out and run away. Not the rabbit but me. Couldn't bear anything near. Any living creature inducing fight or flight instincts. Panic, threat, attack. A pacifist at heart, a natural course of action to run. The capacity to engage or connect with outer phenomena beginning to appear untenable. Becoming an objective observer. An alien in the room. Unseen, unknown, but unable to make known and peer out of the cocoon that rendered me imprisoned.

Josh had problems from early on. Evidently. He alluded to leaving home and packing his bags. Pushing Mother off a cliff in her wheelchair. Not that she had one. The word 'psycho' came to mind; and that is how I would refer to him. Unsure how that word came into my psyche but it was. His rants and rage, the level of anger and hatred far beyond the situation dictated. Fearing for my life. He could kill. The dart in the face was a good one. Ninety degrees below my eye. Had to pull it out myself. 'Lobbing and cobbing', launching and projecting missiles daily, as routine. Anything attainable within arms reach. Knives, bottles, stones, instruments, implements, anything and everything. Always belligerent and pernicious.

The class allocated, post-separation from Josh was okay in principle. But the chair and desk delegated adjacent to the most abrasive, bitter, nasty girl. Lisa. A perfect match, predator and prey. She would get her kicks through insults. Throwing the work-book on the floor, I'd retrieve it, then she'd flick on the floor again, the cycle would repeat. Before long, falling behind with work. Break-time had arrived and noted well behind and deserved to be detained for poor effort. Mrs Moseley, the current teacher, ignorant to my traits and character. Excruciatingly shy, reserved, quiet, and elective mute. A tenacious hard worker, never got behind with anything. Punctuality second to none.

The other pupils were quite impressed. I could spell 'university'. Intelligently advanced. However, a handicap impeded by unidentifiable adversity. Reading was enjoyable. While in the car always observing the immediate environment.

"J & J Sons Ltd!"

"What does that mean Mum? Why Ltd? Why not Limited? Who is J & J? Who are the Sons?"

By the time we had arrived at our destination; consumed every label, billboard, sign, bus advertisement, flyer, pub, football club, cricket ground, speedway, office block and restaurant. Unmentioned bridges passed under that had proverbial graffiti "Sharon + John forever", daubed for all to see. The elected method of learning about the world, to spell, and understand the environment. An objective observer.

We did go to the library in class and get a couple of books out each week. Failing to finish a book, more than that, never really got started. It seemed my retention of text or information was shot. Failing to digest, stick or mean anything. My enthusiasm soon waned, un-fulfilling, un-stimulating, and missing satisfaction. Although I did enjoy the concept of reading. Another dichotomy. Able but unable. Ably incapacitated. Competent but inhibited. School work acceptable for my years. But would look at what others were writing, how they approached the topic, style of their hand writing. The way they formed their f's, p's and t's. Unbelieving own ability. Somehow counterfeit.

Josh and I were almost forced into wearing the same clothes. I guess, we'd look lovely and sweet. Didn't really bother me: easy-going and could accommodate whatever the scenario. He'd be outraged, furious, adamantly inconceivable to occur. Wouldn't leave the house in the same clothes, or seen anywhere near. Never got the idea of being one half of two. Fifty per cent of one. One of two halves. Demanded independence. We selected our own clothes when asked. Always opting for a premium brand or a nice shiny bright logo, emblem or label. Shiny metallic or primary colours. If two pairs and one diffused, bland, or neutral in colour, avoided. My tendency towards notably vibrant, distinguished, regal, and reverent colour almost military in stature: illuminating.

A poignant issue in Jack's life. A sense of marred, scarred, greyed, or blackened. The bright, shiny, premium brand attempting to portray; a counter-attack or antidote to the enemy within.

We would walk to school daily. But not of Josh's choosing. If he could possibly say,
"I won't walk with him. I'll go alone," he would.

But that would have been ridiculous even to his own logic. So he endured; suffered me and resented it. And boy did I pay. Beginning with a lead or pole position, at least three to four metres. Failing to close the gap, the greater pace and increment to catch up, the faster he would walk to maintain the distance and ultimately escape. His demeanour and body language spoke volumes. Contempt, belligerent, vitriolic. Bewildered at my unknown crime. Implausible to speak, the signals well versed. A truism. Unwilling to be seen with me or even associated. Passing in the corridor, unacknowledged, failing to glance my way. This went on week after week, month after month. Daring to speak or even comment would render me lambasted and shot down with a torrent of verbal abuse. Swore at and told where to take myself. Stopping to tie a shoelace, continuing to walk and forsake me, uncaring. Wanted the security of having a companion for support but not to be alone. But at the same time resented it was me.

As well as dinner lady, Mother had been a Sales Representative. It wasn't long before she left the dinner-lady position to become Sales Manager. Shortly followed by a trip to Rome; not of her own volition but work. We were staying with her mother; our Nan and her second husband Reginald. It didn't feel good, as with all the other situations we were left. Never feeling safe or close to them. Just people to be dropped off with when an inconvenience occurred. Rather work and adult socialisation took priority. It was yet another example left prematurely without consent.

On the school's six-weeks holiday, shipped off to Nan's. Commonly a stressful expedition getting there. Mother fraught with tension. Desperate to get there to get back for some chore or legalistic daily agenda she had contrived, void of flexibility or concession. The dishes, hang the washing out, hoover, all before heading off to work. If the bus was coming we'd have to run for it. Unthinkable, to wait patiently for the next one. Life or death. We must get this one at all cost. Panic and despair a common experience. Once off the bus we'd have to walk through the park to get to Nan's. At a fast pace, uncaring whether we were following or not. Invariably left behind. On the odd occasion she might bump into someone then okay for her to stand and talk. Excluded from conversation and missing an introduction to the individual.

Once at Nan's ushered into the living room to watch the TV and be quiet. Charles waiting for us. My Uncle Charles' son, young Charles. Uncle Charles was Mother's brother. Primed before reception on arrival. Phoning our house that morning to remind us he was unwell, or a headache and should be noted. Also, be especially quiet not to exacerbate it. Feeling a nuisance and a burden. That was our position. The submissive poor side of the family. Condescending, disparaging, and arrogant, assuming a position of superiority and authority. We were the sub-relatives.

On entering Nan's we'd be told:

"Take your shoes off! Don't tread there, move that, touch that, or spill anything. Be quiet!"

Always in the wrong by default; guilty for breathing. Constantly overruled undermined and belittled.

Reg was an absolute arse-hole. Already estranged from his only son, divorced, now Mother's step-dad. Dad would collect us after work. He'd finish about 2 p.m. Up about 4.30 a.m, a delivery driver for Baxters, a local bakery. Unspoken and unacknowledged on arrival, meandering in. Like we weren't even there. Then after coffee and a smoke we'd be returned back home. Again, silence all the way home. Missing:

"How's your day been? What have you been up to?"

An abyss.

When not at Nan's, left to our own devices. Mother disengaged. Therefore making work of light hands. Entertained ourselves by whatever means deemed fit at the time. Up to no good. We'd often meander down to the local railway line. There, resided a rectangle cavity between the line about four feet by two and two feet deep. Self-inspired plan, getting down there; crouching and lowering myself in when the train passed over. All attention-seeking. I never did it in the end. A possibility. Exploring old dilapidated factory buildings with precarious floors and ceilings of a bygone age. Regularly lighting fires. In fact, one Sunday afternoon Mum and Dad were sleeping on the couch. We were left to it. Josh took it upon himself to set alight the bed clothes in his bedroom. Then, come tells us the house is on fire. Bearing a smug grin, fused with guilt and and awareness of wrongdoing. Almost wanting to be found-out. Fortunately, something and nothing. More a cry for help: attention-seeking. The offending artefact, a mere six-inch^2 piece of blanket, blackened and toast-like, scorched and burnt. We were obsessed with it. We'd love to watch the flickering flames, the heat and life they exhibited, and embers glow. Wade through streams, collect frog spawn, dissect legs, collect birds' eggs, build dams in the brook. On occasion Dad's Mum would house-sit for us. Mum would recruit her to do the cleaning and housework as she was too busy and Nan could double up and care for us at the same time. Since Josh and I had been going to school for several years with the same children off the estate, our acquaintances shared. All same age, from the same few streets attending same school. Regularly showing off; readily degraded and denigrated in public or in front of acquaintances to extol his superior virtue. Making it abundantly publicly known of my sub-position and his superior position. Only on this occasion took it too far. In the living room, exercising his authority in front of this acquaintance. The next thing prostrate on the deck; face down. Restrained. Then took an almighty jump up in the air and landed on the middle of my back. That was it. Couldn't breathe; thought I was going to die there and then. Inhaling but negligible oxygen reaching my lungs. Another gasp but nothing again. This went on for about thirty seconds. But eventually the constriction abated, slowly able to breathe again. Nan was another impersonal, emotionally incapacitated family member, distant and aloof. Absent in skills of expressing love, care or spiritual, emotional nourishment. Running in to tell her of my ordeal. She gave me a shot of whiskey.

The educational school culture of the day was one of punitive correction. A tick or an "x". Good or bad. My teacher would use guilt to persuade or motivate.

"Are you going to be one of those people with a fag hanging out of their mouth?"

A vacuum of praise, affirmation or approval of any kind. The undercurrents and attitude to learning was:

"Must do better!"
"Must try harder!"
"Must work longer!"
"There is no such word as can't!"

If you managed to do all of these things then criticism could be avoided. That was all. I had a male teacher at the age of ten, Mr Dunn. Revering him as some kind of role model or patriarchal figure. Athletic and managed football coaching. The images still vivid. Painting a picture of a hump-back bridge. We studied bridges and engineering, Isambard Kingdom Brunel. Loved it; in my element. However, the painting unsuccessful in reaching the pinnacle of approval. All occupied but for a spare 2mm space where I could possibly paint anymore. But a case of:
"Go back and do more, still more you need to do!"
"No, it's still not complete!" he would recite.

One day glancing at my watch unbeknown Mr Dunn stood directly behind.

"Only ten minutes to lunch guys!" I said to my fellow contemporaries at the table.

Mr Dunn quickly responded:

"Yeah, that's about right for you Jack, isn't it?" insinuating a loser persona, work-shy, indolent and slothful, with ill repute.

Wasn't the words so much but tone and sentiment behind it. Real, intense, purposeful. Meant with punishing, persecuting perniciousness. Devastated. Guilt and badness resonated through. Bad.

It didn't matter whether the painting met its finality. Mother didn't have things like that in the house; rendered untidy. She had already disposed of anything and everything we had ever created or produced from kindergarten. The clay figures hand-made, set in the kiln, glossed over. The bats made out of fabric and stuffing for Halloween. The drawings, sketches, written work. All binned. This painting could have gone in the National Art Gallery, but no.

I loved painting. An opportunity to go on a school trip to the Sheffield Museum. However, only a handful of children permitted. Those that had the best painting. Unknown criteria; only the best can go. Invested heart and soul into creating this piece of art. Un-elected of the chosen few. Apparently, mine didn't fill the whole paper.
The third year of Junior school; Mr Whately my teacher now. A relatively old man in the teacher age range. About late fifties I'd say. On commencement of the new academic year we'd have to write about the six-week's holidays; done or not done. Good at writing and possessed a creative adventurous mind to complement. Not that commendations, positive feedback or superlatives had been received over the years. But fully aware. However, this hidden talent wouldn't be used in the way intended. The events or non-events that occurred over the summer went un-chronicled. My imagination used to concoct a fantasy story. Fiction. Basically attention seeking. Crossing the line in terms of school rules, acceptability and morality. Delving into realms of rudeness. Using metaphors; not to give the game away. Without elaborating, explicitly succinct, getting away with it. About balls and pubic hair. Mr Whately's would remark on my work, "A rather strange story."

Moreover, unrelated to the story but motive and provocation behind it. Suffering neglect; abandonment and abject alienation. A cry for help. To be noticed. Wanting to be caught out or punished; therefore seen. To reinforce this view other immoral behaviours exhibited which could be construed as strange. On an evening Mum and Dad would have gone out or visiting; left alone in the house. Rifling through the phone book; discover Mr Whately's home phone number and ring it. A prank call. Only to put the phone down again. The proverbial 'house points system' practised to reward good behaviour. Sure, most of the kids made them up. I was too honest. Confessing each week, "Five, sir!" The others anything up of twenty-five, even forty or fifty. Funny, how teachers were unheard the whole week through granting them to anyone. But somehow come Friday afternoon an abundance of house points would reveal themselves. Always tried my best; went the extra mile. The number of doors held open; unyielding manners and politeness that went unnoticed. The helpfulness attempting to portray. Anyway, it seemed Mr Whately had taken notice. Awarded title of Best Pupil as I'd worked uncompromisingly diligently all day. Flabbergasted at this incredulous announcement. The exhilaration that ascended my spirit unprecedented. Someone noticed.

Unannounced on the second period of Tuesday afternoon, told to join Mr Jenkins' class next door. The period turned out to be some kind of geography quiz. Exceptionally keen to do well in games or quizzes. Devouring the attention and being the 'Best', a winner. It backfired sometimes. Last year in fact, in my lower year playing charades. Unable to contain myself; knowing the clue, even though my inner voice yelling not to make a fool of myself. It'll be wrong, then you'll look stupid. The exuberance and zeal conquered. Shock, horror, got the damn bloody thing right; spot on. "Woo hoo!!! Oh shit!" Elated, giddy, astonished and happy for a split second. Fused with fear of impending overwhelming attention, in direct cross-hair focus of the class and teacher.

"The person that gets it has to stand up at the front and present their charade" said Miss.

My nemesis: overwhelmed by attention. My anxieties kicked in; with it worry, fear and self doubt; mind going to mush. The stress quelled any creative flair I might have stored up. Mumbling, fluffing, glowing bright red; a regular occurrence. They knew I was struggling and out of my depth. I knew that they knew that I knew. Pleading inside, somebody bloody get it, save me the pain. Sooner or later somebody did get it to great relief.

But Mr Jenkins gave a clue in the geography quiz,
"You will find this place at forty five degrees!"
Got it ... Anglesey!

He was so impressed, commended me and said Mr. Whately had some outstanding pupils. Sensing an overwhelming sensation unacquainted before. Internal jubilation, triumphant excitement, palpable heart beat, positivity, giddy and not too embarrassed or red-faced to receive the compliment. Happy albeit temporarily.

Josh and Paul always ahead of me socially. At ten attending work with Dad, up at 4:30, down to the bakery, helping out as much as a ten year old could. A passenger or 'van-lad' while Dad drove to his customers delivering that day's bread and confectionery. Void of stimulus at home. Mother investing time and energy in domestic chores, sweeping, gardening, ironing, cleaning, and visiting friends. The loneliness and isolation setting in. How much more could one self-stimulate? Do jigsaws alone, watch TV for hours and hours. The outcome, to join them commencing work with Dad. But premature. Too much of a little child, undeveloped. But what else could I do, between a rock and a hard place? A terrifying experience. The night before, unable to sleep; worried about the pending morning. Visualising and prophesying how the day would reveal itself. Probably wake before the alarm, pre-emptive, prepared, and hyper vigilant. Once washed and dressed adorning the yellow company standard overall with respective name emblazoned. Dad typically mute. Missing "Good morning!". From waking to arriving at work, absence of words were exchanged or expressed. The worry and anxiety would continue unabated. The frenetic activity and mêlée that ensued would compound an already perplexed disposition. Obviously, unspoken merely attempting to retain my composure and cope with the internal distress, overwhelmed by the social environment. All grown men, hardened, cold, stereotypical Sheffield men and working-class. The social etiquette one of berating, mocking, and factory floor banter. Swearing, shouting, arguing; a raucous. Knowingly out of my depth. Untimely. Unprepared and ill equipped. All too intimidating. But what could I do?

Travelling to Butlins this year for the family annual holiday. Mild contention from Charles Senior, as apparently Pontins was materially superior. Butlins at the lower end of the market and not as good apparently. Josh, Paul, and Charles Junior would explore the camp, go to wherever the moment took them; rides, slots, amusements, and dodgems. Tagging along, but that's all it was. If I had not followed abandonment would have prevailed. Seldom included or speaking as though absent. Randomly visiting the parents in the bar to touch base, then off again as kids did. Remember thinking, no one has enquired about my needs, how I am; what I'd like to do, drink, food, sufficient money. Absolute alienation. Unseen unknown.

Ironically, made aware via Mother and circumvented by Dad.

"Your Dad has said what a nice lad you're turning out to be!"
"Oh right!" I replied, puzzled.

Bewildered that Dad was unspoken, but the moment he decides to pay his unprecedented inaugural approval it's via someone else. "Terriffic!" Making a mental note of how bizarre even this was, had sealed it. Dad was never going to relate directly. Only a proxy relationship via Mother.

We were untouched. A huge void and absence of affection, consolation, and reassuring support. Never a hug; nor would they hold our hand. Missing a pat on the shoulder for affirmation. Void. Upon greeting, failing to greet, say, "Hello, how are you?" or acknowledge. Merely floating around merging into the situation. Again, on departure absent physical contact. Mum would at least shout from the bottom of the stairs, "We're off out!" or from another room. Dad circumvented around it. Already sat in the car waiting to leave. That's how it was. Never were we informed; he was going and that we'd see him soon; giving eye contact. Annulled. He would periodically have a week off work. A regular six week cycle; working six days. Arriving home from school for lunch. But on entering the house, failing to turn around, greet, acknowledge, or speak at all. Eating in heavy silence; missing enquiry, what have you done today? How is it going? Void. The odd occasion whereby we'd go to the local swimming pool as a family. Being kids, all good fun; splashing, jumping, racing, grabbing each other. Leaping on Dad in a moment of impulse. But within a split second, deflected and rejected physically as though a volley ball. Instantaneously in shock, perplexed. My body sensing had been pierced by lethal injection. Synonymous to the Amazonian Bullet Ants. The sting of the Bullet Ant is said to be the most painful of any sting and is compared to being hit by a bullet. This poison would permeate my entire being. Stunned and annulled. For moments in a daze, my mind disoriented; confused. Isn't that what you do as a kid; jump on your dad? That was my Dad wasn't it? I am his son, aren't I? What the fuck! A seed had been sown. Scarred. My Dad doesn't want me anywhere near him.

The kids on the street became our surrogate parents. The older ones, our neighbours kids that used to babysit for us. Five or six years our senior. Taking us to the swimming baths; our silent opaque chaperones. We tagged along a lot. In fact some nasty girls resented us following, because they liked the boys;

would brand us ‘sheep’. A follower: speaking would be superfluous—done for me.

My first spending money ever. Fifty pence. A summers day and the ice-cream man had just turned up. A wonderful experience to buy something with my own money; which was desirable. Electing for a ‘King Kong’ lolly with toffee inside and hundreds and thousands on the outer, coated in chocolate. Within minutes Dad saw me:

“Have you just spent all of your pocket money on that?”

I replied, “Yes!” with a curious vulnerable innocence. Thinking wasn’t that what it was for.

Dad responded, “Bloody idiot!”

We didn’t get treats. Unlike most kids on the estate. We’d have to go without. Often at the shops we’d ask to have this or that, but no. Unknown, uninformed about our hobbies or interests, what made us happy; drink, food, music, or toy stimulated our mind or emotions. Just fed, watered, and given enough to survive on.

The marriage of HRH Prince Charles and Princess Lady Diana, July 1981. A street party celebration was organised on our street. Music, balloons, banners, food, drink, bunting, a very British affair. A hot July summers day. Perfect for the occasion. Although an ominous poignant moment. The chairs in the garden organised in such a way, forming a crescent shape or semi-circle. The arched side facing me. In some ways unvexed but familiar. Exclusive, left out on the periphery. But also visually strong and forceful, symbolic and metaphorical. All seats occupied; missing a vacancy, absent entry points to this private affair, or inner-sanctum. The outside felt very real, alone, excluded and banished. While living this moment of perplexity, confused, disillusioned, and disoriented. A neighbour noted the scar on my fore-arm.

"What have you done there, Jack?"
Taken aback in surprise that I had been seen. Immediately ashamed that I've been found out, discovered. But not for what I'd achieved—rather the opposite.

"Errrrmm … what mark on my arm?"
"That one there!" she quizzed.

"Oh just something I had done at school!" said with great embarrassment, stupidity, and self-loathing.

We had a thing at school at the time whereby one would scratch oneself ninety-nine times if not more to irritate the skin: gnaw away until an open wound. In retrospect probably a tribal mark to define one's place in a community. Acknowledging these kids had dysfunctional, abusive homes, neglected. The first signs devoid of self-worth. A merciless carelessness. A visual milestone, evidenced by a scar.

Striving to be noticed were sown as seeds and rooted in my soul. Must excel, strive, aiming for approval and acceptance; number one; the best. We'd go swimming with school weekly. A natural good strong swimmer for my age; despite the débâcle earlier in my life with the arm-bands fiasco. Unbeknown, they had deemed this session a race. A local press photographer present and in the local edition of the Chronicle. Only three of us in the race. But prior to start decided it was mine. Life or death. In the bag. Exerting all energies as though the swim of my life. Won no problem. Swimming to the edge and the steps to depart the pool when met by the press photographer. Unsure what he said; guessing he asked my name. The conclusion: logical that my photo and name blazoned all over the local paper. Blank. Not a whisper. Only that our school had been to the pool and an image showing all the kids sat down in front of it. Unmentioned of my winning or name.

Unattended at Sports Day. "Too busy working". A surreal moment having dozens of excitable mums and dads, aunties, and uncles waiting in anticipation of their child; niece or nephew partaking in their first egg-and-spoon race or two laps of the athletics track. Perplexed of the motive and purpose. If missing so-called loved ones, guardians, or relatives that know me. The teachers; parents of the other kids unacquainted. What is it all about? Why would I even begin to race? Sorrowful and bewildered. Confused at best.

Parents' evening much the same: another farce. We've got teachers that don't know me and parents that don't know me, that are going to have a discussion of which I am not privy; the conclusion of which is never imparted. Returning while playing on the street, in their absence. Obviously, you'd be desperate for feedback. How did I do? Any good? Good?, Bad?, Average? Missing a smile, frown, elevated facial expression, or raised eyebrow. Void.

We were all bed-wetters. Having to visit a clinic attempting to diagnose the root cause. In my innate intuition, I knew. This is what happens to children that are neglected, worriers; anxious and nervous. Because of insecurity, unsafe and instability. From homes missing structure, care affection: certainty and routine. But more than that... Missing Love. Makes sense.

Fishing became the mainstay or staple interest. One of our mutual friends and I would walk to the local dam about a quarter of a mile away. We'd leave home about 5:30 a.m, arrive at the bank just before dawn; six-ish. By this time we'd cobbled together sufficient know-how, either by watching and learning or trial and error. Our tied hooks were never perfect. They'd stay while piercing bait, such as maggots for instance. But as soon as you'd caught the fish of considerable size and weight, invariably pulling out, you lost not only the hook but also the specimen.

Dad once took us to another venue, a huge reservoir. Allowed to have a go; seemingly mentoring, informing, "When you get a bite, hit it!" I did, well, what I thought was a strike. But realistically more of a slow drag.

"What was that? Pathetic!" said Dad with a critical disappointed tone.

A few years later at Nan's over the holidays fishing at the pond in the park. Viewing a shoal of large chub from my peg, as the water was so shallow. Low and behold hooked onto one; became the focal point and centre of attention for all those nearby. Self-proclaimed hero off the day— or so I thought. My biggest fish. A one pound chub. But as with everything that had amassed, was achieved or produced. Glossed over, quashed or dumbed down to the point of irrelevance. The elation and excitement fleeting. Charles Junior, Josh and Paul had had enough of my glory and self-adulation. On returning back to Nan's, still giddy. Couldn't wait to tell Dad I'd caught the biggest fish between everyone. The 'self acclaimed fisherman of the day!'. How proud and happy I was. Synonymous to getting the charades right and the Anglesey quiz with Mr Jenkins correct. Enlivened with abundant joy, in high spirits, excited, fulfilled and satisfied.

"Oh right!"
"Hhhmmmm!"
"Aarrhhh!"

That was it. Null and void. Zero superlatives, un-affirmed, un-recognised and unapproved. Inanimate facially, just glossed over; uneventful.

My reasons for striking improperly were due to toiling too hard; not to over do it or yank the bloody line and float so hard and fast that it would end up in the trees; in the banking at our rear. Over compensating, striving hard to try not to. Similarly, if I did speak, exceptionally quiet, a whisper. If I say it soft enough when unheard it's not going to be so devastating; half expecting they didn't hear anyway.

When at home, left to wander wherever life may lead us. Going together but a strange dynamic. Following was the norm. Knowing, unwelcome, despised, and resented. His dichotomy, enduring a perceived adversary but undesirable to be alone either. Basically tolerated my presence. Only a case of time before un-willfully stepping over the dreaded line, which didn't take much. Said the inappropriate word: in his head anyway. Over shot my position. The abuse often excessive and certainly undeserving of the situation. My comments invariably humorous or sarcastic, but seldom malicious. On meandering around the local park something must have kicked off. I'd committed another Sin or uttered an unlawful impediment to his dislike. Sending me home again. A regular occurrence. Once he'd had enough or couldn't bear the sight anymore. Ordered home, disobedient. An assault of bricks, sticks, missiles, kicks and punches till submission. Seemingly, a traumatic event to be ordered somewhere, against ones choosing. Rejected, ostracised and forced, missing rights. But so believable, common everyday occurrence. It wasn't strange but predictable and the norm. The horror would mitigate via its frequency and re-occurrence. Therefore, emotions or thoughts went like. I know the drill, here we go again. Confused, bewildered, sad, disappointed, hurt and lonely.

Unimaginable about to unfold next... far beyond anything witnessed prior. Inhaling through his nose to gain as much phlegm as possible, cleared his throat, and spat an horrendous mouthful of spit and saliva in my face. Running down and over my nose and mouth. Stunned and annulled in a split second, in-shock. Grief and feelings of gross degradation, inhumanity and humiliation resonated throughout my mind and body. Beyond emotions, more like shock. Unable to cry, it was beyond crying. In a state of intransigence. To fight, flee, retort or regain composure, assess and analyse what had just occurred. A horrific harrowing event. Fully aware a line had been breached. A holocaust moment. The sense of betrayal, stooping to such a level of abuse for something so innocuous I can't even remember. A proportion of 'rape'. Breaching human rights, soul-destroying. Only a few weeks prior at the same location. The local park, minding our own business. Stood with our bikes. An unknown suspect began sprinting at speed in direct line to where I stood. Synonymous to an African lion confronting its prey. The closer, his intentions became more definite. As with the lion's prey its a case of how long do I wait before legging-it? Gauging; 'Recceing' accomplished and confirmed heading for me and at my neck in precisely ten seconds. A prescient time to do one. Gooooooooo!!!!! Hadn't the faintest conviction what the hell I had done to deserve an unwarranted wanton attack. Just for being, bait or predatory prey.

Another annual holiday; to Scotland this time. We'd purchased a touring caravan now. As usual, the 'long silence' driving up there. Good times were experienced. Camped close to the lochs: fishing, walks, light nights up to 10 p.m in the evening and great weather. The natural outstanding beauty that surrounded us, mountains, rivers, lochs, and scenery. Awesome.

However, the chronological milestones in Jack's life would re-surface on this holiday. He had developed a phobia of wind, unbeknown to him. Due to the heat and long sunny days quite plausible to have the windows open in the car. A catalyst for trauma. Any gust of wind or freak breeze would take his breath away, rendered hyperventilating. Rigidly stiff with fear. Literally terrified. Seemingly, a metaphor for losing control. The erratic, fickle and variable nature of wind would yield a sense of 'vexed'. Sometimes occurring if the car suddenly went in a dip in the road too quickly, when your heart drops a beat. Vacant consolation. Even the level of distress, agitation, overwhelmed, whaling, crying, and sobbing his heart out. They failed to minister to turn around or close the windows either.

Innumerable attempts were made to speak to Mum but she didn't understand. Diffused, dumbed down, and dismissed. "Don't worry about it!" she'd say. I did worry. Freaked me out. The fear greater than death itself. In fact, often thought better to be shot right here right now than to go through this harrowing experience. Unknown, void of compassion, suffering as an orphan.

WHITE BLANK PAGE

We grew up with the telly. First thing in a morning: on. As soon as we had walked through the door after school: on. Babysitters: on. The main focal point of the living room and family life. Left on our own: on. Transfixed. An omission of dialogue and discourse, as the TV took centre stage. Attempting to express myself but informed,

"But we're watching this! But we can't hear it!"
"But Dad is trying to listen to this programme!"

Even better at Christmas, when the grandparents and relatives came over. After Christmas dinner; five solid hours of silence. Glaring into space. Either James Bond or Doctor Zhivago. Void of stimulus that would yield us an environment to flourish or discover our inner talents. Left with the TV for entertainment. Although Josh and I were once ushered to the local Boy's Brigade, again before our time. Unsupported, social, moral or otherwise. Unsurprisingly, it didn't last. Unconnected or had the self-esteem or confidence to socialise.

Christmas was crap. Fair enough, receiving everything requested. But absent people. Annulled of personal input; indifferent with our games or toys. You played alone. Visitors speaking between themselves. The customary dutifully written cards like all the bygone years. But missing companion or friend to share Christmas.

Jack had migrated from Junior school to Secondary; comp. Bringing with him everything gleaned and weaned: knowledge, experience, conditioning, culture, and etiquette. Doubt, fear, worry, paranoia, and confusion. Friends, absent. Migrating alone. Jack put into 'Disc' group and Josh 'Over'. Naturally gravitating towards the other child delinquents of the cohort. Fatherless, bed-wetters, sourced from other dysfunctional homes and social depravity. Seemingly, an attractive option, given the other spectrum of 'Swots'; respectably attired, well spoken, intelligent kids. His potential unrealised. A paradigm shift or universal about-change exists in the ethos from Junior to Secondary school. His precious hidden traits subdued. In an environment unrecognised by name or looks, notwithstanding deep-rooted abilities.

During P.E, a volunteer support worker addressed me as 'Jeff Bridges!' Familiarity taught me to receive any spoken word as callous, slanderous, insulting, or abusive. Notwithstanding the shock of being 'seen' momentarily. Stunned: unable to compose myself.

Who the hell is Jeff Bridges? pelted across my mind in desperation to qualify this assertion.
An elephant man type figure?
An ugly hunch-back of a Notre Dame figure?

Thoughts whizzed back and forth in my consciousness, endeavouring to avail of ridicule yet again. Assuming the worst, yet another dig. Disparaging, diluting, and denigrating. My ignorance or naivety led to interpreting or receiving negatively; thinking someone else wants to have a pop at me. Unthinkable he might have been charismatic, good looking, a highly revered global actor with innumerable accolades and commendations to his name.

Rare glimmers of potential unobtrusively surfaced but went unnoticed. Having invested effort and succeeded delivering a comprehensive piece of work then to have modest approval didn't cut it to motivate further. If there is little or no reward for effort, then what's the point?

My school report would depict me as a 'day-dreamer', in a world of my own. Lost, staring. A dearth of enquiries; how I felt or thought about anything. The desire to discover the underlying problem. This was the Eighties. A view reinforced with the incident with Mrs Fraser, the history teacher. So lost and perplexed, who and what I was doing here: what it all meant in a world of my own. When Mrs Fraser, not known for her subtle pedagogical approach, came at me like a bolt of lightning. Knowing what was coming the moment her facial expression altered, became red-faced bubbling with rage. The rocking of my chair on two legs was the offending occupation. My head had pre-empted and fantasised that I'd be rebuked for using two legs instead of four. However, in the midst of being disillusioned with life, lost in my head, my response was what it was.

"How many legs does that chair have?" she yelled.
"Two Miss!"
"How many?"
The volume and tone increasing, fused with anger.
"Two Miss!" I responded fearfully sheepish.
"How many?"
The volume and tone increasing even greater, tempered with further anger and frustration.

By this time it crossed my mind all was unwell. A quick wake-up call and the error was revealed.
"Errr—four, Miss!"

Viewed as the class idiot, stupid at best. But no teacher, parent or pupil would know my mental or emotional state. Void of feeling. Numb, passive to the extreme, lost and unknown by any human-being. The very class that Josh and I shared the same teacher and subject. Mrs Fraser marking the homework of the previous week in front of us during the current lesson. All of a sudden she pops up:

"What's this all about? I've just read this once!", she questioned, indignant with rage, sifting through all the previous books she had just marked.

"Who's been copying?"
It was my book she was holding up.
"Jack, this is yours. Have you been copying?"

I knew full well I hadn't. Granted, prevalent issues with envy and jealousy; thinking everyone did everything better, spoke, wrote, sung, drew or played. But an innocent copier. The identical copy was Josh's. He exhibited an embarrassing grin on his face. Then rapturous laughter took over the whole class by the contemporary pupil bystanders. The conspiracy exposed; guilty for seeking my book out at home clandestinely: copied it word for word. Too obstinate to ask for help. Unwilling to do that. Too proud to submit, experience vulnerability, and request for a legitimate need to be met. No. Had to avoid and commit the act incognito and surreptitiously.

Within weeks of attending, Jack was smoking with the other smokers, sharing identical broken homes. That's what happens. Two damaged, lost, broken individuals find each other. You feel more at home mirrored by someone of a similar ilk. Attending the proverbial rear of the 'bike sheds', for a fag at break—although a newly built sports centre with 'Astroturf'. Spending his dinner money to buy a pack of ten. Through the smoking acquaintance, introduced to a wider 'gang'. His dad asleep on arrival home from school: Mum at work. So a quick bread-and-jam sandwich then off out. Having accepted the position in life as orphaned runt, his role and purpose in life based on that. Lost in a group. Unattached and aloof. As the other attendees had issues and were also vying for their place in the world or role in the gang. They would keep him submissive and inferior for their own self-preservation. A daily routine to mock, insult, and verbally abuse. Find the smallest of error, most trivial scope for culpability, to justify condemnation. All he knew and would passively accept as his role. Physical kicking and punching would compound an already indisposed being; when it suited.

One day having a fag behind the sports hall the deputy headmaster walked around to catch everyone. Absent cigarettes on me neither was I smoking. Cash-less or no means to acquire any. Standing vacant, while the others more innovative puffed away. He asked to turn my pockets out. A lighter revealed. Confiscating and noted if I wanted it back I should go to his office later that day. Twelve years old and naive the intuition didn't save me this time. The worst mistake I had made. He threatened me physically, that if he caught me again he'd knock me from pillar to post. Sending a letter home to Mother on what was happening. We used to go home for lunch. We had keys. Josh knew I had torn it up and put it in the bin. But wasn't an ally. Gloating with glee, knowing he'd get me into more trouble and couldn't wait for the suffering and punitive correction. The inevitable happened. Informing Mum. She punished by preventing me from going out with the gang anymore. Missing any other acquaintances, that was it. My life over. Remaining in the house every evening until I left school at sixteen. An omission of compensation, consolation, or alternative stimulus to meet anyone else. To join a club or get involved in an activity, hobby or interest that I enjoyed. She would write back to the deputy headmaster and tell him the story. He would then punish some more. Josh wallowing in his gleeful euphoria; I had suffered once more to his credit. The irony—none of them actually knew anything about me. Who I was, abilities, views, skills, intrinsic traits, or life experiences. All missed it. Hook, line, and sinker.

Fishing had become my thing. At every given opportunity I'd want to be fishing. Whether the solace, peace and quiet, nature, or just people-less. We weren't given money for anything. If I wanted a fishing licence, bait, floats, line, and hooks, I'd have to find it myself. This motivated me to keep going down to the bakery as stand-in van-lad. Despite my reservations of being uncomfortable in a predominately male working-class environment, whereby pilloried, ridiculed, and disparaging references made towards one were the norm. The fishing I wanted.

The school had organised a week long trip for our year. An outward-bound, pot-holing, abseiling, and walking expedition. Exploring the local countryside and heritage in Derbyshire. Intending to imbue some maturity and independence in the children. We'd have to make our own sandwiches and pack lunches, cook in the evening, wash up, and general domestic duties. Staying in a dormitory. Keen to go. Right up my street: adventure. Boys' stuff. Freedom to muck about with the other lads, surreptitiously, and have a fag away from the teachers. Generally get up to no good. Ambivalent about my feelings. Did I miss home? What is missing? I feel sad. Is that what it is? Do I miss them or just the familiar surroundings? Is this what they call home-sick?

Unspoken for the majority of the week. Quite perplexed and lost. Did a lot of following and copy-cat stuff. But the perennial lack of human connection would pervade. Unthinkable to speak to teachers. Either a fear of rejection, rebuke, denial, or merely feeling a burden. The ability to establish connections beyond the temporal with the other kids didn't bear fruit either. An insidious spiritual phenomenon that would always outwit. The week passed uneventfully. We had accomplished and complied with our agenda for the week. Now it was down to the return journey and how the pending reception would prevail upon arrival. Given that by now wouldn't be picked up from the coach at school. Having this experience so many times before. Whether a day trip or just a local affair. Expected that I'd make my own way home. Awful to see the other kids' parents and guardians so enthusiastic, couldn't wait to see their Johnny. Passionate to discover, had they enjoyed it? What was the best bit? What did you do? I'd have to walk home with my bags alone. On arrival, void of communication. Blended into the décor and environment seamlessly. Missing a single reference or enquiry of where I had been all week, experiences enjoyed, discoveries made, lessons learnt or enjoyment attained. Zilch.

Through the school's six-weeks holiday I might work for five of those weeks. Six days per week. Assigned to a loathsome driver, Joe. Arriving for work over an hour late with me dripping wet in sweat, aiming to do my level best; fearful of any criticism, rejection or insult. Excusing himself; exhausted after digging the foundations to the new annexe of his home. Sensing and almost smelling his cruel intentions like a creature that senses its predator at a distance. Rendered more reserved. Still unsafe. Openly humiliating and gleefully degrading in public, exclaiming, "The quiet man!" or "Silent man!" in front of shopkeepers, staff, and colleagues. A big laugh to him. I'd do all the heavy lifting and carrying, again dripping in sweat. He'd stand there nonchalantly writing the invoice; talking to staff. Five pounds for nine hours. The more abusive, more muted I'd become. The more ashamed; and so the self-loathing would ensue. Unsympathetic from parents or anyone. Informed to take no notice; as my consoling reassurance.

Desperate for some waders. Ionic for fishermen. If wearing waders, you were the consummate fisherman. 'You da man!' Missing a white knight that would buy them for me. Only eleven pounds. Taking eighteen months, working the odd weekend, the random school holiday, forking out for maggots, floats, and line in-between. Eventually a momentous occasion. The sum of eleven pounds had accumulated. Now possible to purchase my first prized, coveted waders.

We did well for holidays. Travelling around the country in a touring caravan. We'd have great boys' adventures stymied by the family dysfunction. On this occasion, in Lincolnshire close to the River Witham; another fishing holiday. Towards the latter of the holiday a pain had developed between my legs: rendered walking like John Wayne or someone with Rickets. First thing back, Monday morning at the 'Docs'.

Upon examination he thought I should go to the Hospital for a further assessment. We arrived at the ward, circumventing out-patients. He did say, "Take a bag in case!" Unexpected to be kept in. Gutted. The childrens ward too. Twelve years old but maturity so much senior. The adult ward would have been more amenable. The children had typical conditions: tonsillitis: appendicitis, broken arms, and legs. But mine so private and personal.

"What are you in for?"
I froze.
"Errrm... not sure!" a timidly inhibited reply.

Breaking down at the bedside. Mother was leaving me to it. Dad was at work so that was it. Still crying as she left. Later that day, Dad would turn up with my brothers and Charles Junior. They'd congregate at the foot of my bed and talk between themselves.

Another annual vacation we would go abroad to Brittany, France. We'd spend two weeks there. Although we had our children's French phrase book. Void of impetus or stimuli to develop or practise the language. Therefore redundant. It made matters worse, having a French oral exam on my return to school. Suffice to say, duly criticised and admonished for lack of knowledge having spent two weeks immersed in it. They would often go out into town but I'd rather stay and go fishing at the huge lake on site. A given, now in my head that we were disjointed, disconnected, aloof and separate. The sense of alienation and aloofness apparent wherever we were. Easier if I just stayed home alone. It occurred while fishing this beautiful lake; a place of complete tranquillity undisturbed by humans. Twelve years old, alone, missing a human-being for at least half a mile. Should this be? What if I fell in? Lost my footing? No phone. No screams heard.

By the third year of comp, awarded a free period or whereby one could do 'Activities'. On offer was wind-surfing, computer club, snooker, bowling, and fishing. Obviously I opted for the activity most enthusiastic about in my entire life. For two hours every Thursday we'd venture out to a local venue. Several weeks had elapsed and a challenge suggested; a fishing match. A competition between all the lads. An opportunity of a life-time to shine. My adrenaline pumping just at the thought of it. The euphoria and utopia of arriving first. The best. All my focus and available attention went towards preparation. A recce of the venue for starters. Surveillance of methods, tactics and style. Ensuring my tackle up to date, clean and viable. Mentally and psychologically synonymous to the Olympics, but fishing my local dam. The self-imposed pressure, responsibility bestowed by self. The seriousness of the occasion became palpable: literally life and death. Inevitably the day arrived. The majority of the other lads took their tackle to school to then go on later in the day, after lessons. However, we lived only a quarter of a mile from the venue so would take mine from home. The lads all had their dad's, uncle's, and brothers behind them in support. Watching, encouraging, affirming and exhorting. Me, the waders and I. Dad either asleep or couldn't be bothered. I'd have to go it alone—again. This unintended consequence merely fuelled concurrent self-punishing attitude: merciless, graceless, unforgiving. Must do better. Got to win. Have to be noticed. Surely!

I gave it my all. Mental, physical, emotional, effort, maggots, worms, hemp, sweetcorn and casters. Blood, sweat, and tears: through the lot at it. The result? Null and void. Not a darn thing. Caught a few roach but nothing significant to qualify for any recognition or praise. Back to the drawing board.

Invariably, during any period not at school, the bakery van-lad job would draw me back. Not for the pleasure or satisfaction but most basic tenet: survival. Able at least to buy my own drink when desired. Liberty of choice, control and partial independence in one's life. Treating self an unprecedented event per se. The treat, a tackle-box, new annual fishing licence, bait, and a day ticket.

I'd help Dad out for a week if his van-lad was on holiday. Accepted, and standard now that he wouldn't speak after appearing in the kitchen at home. On awakening to driving the one-mile journey to work; the one-hour journey to the destination and subsequently all day working. Becoming the norm which you took for granted. Incapable or unwilling to introduce me to the shopkeepers. Greeting and acknowledging each other, passing the day's trivialities. He possessed these prized gloves for work. An exceptional pair. Unsure whether leather or what constituted the material; but revered. One went missing. News to me. Informing everyone that I had lost it. Again, circumventing direct association. Communicating via proxy; me 'who dunnit'. The guilt and sense of condemnation took its place in and around me. Adorning like a cloak. At least, if communicated to we could have resolved it there and then. Maybe "Sorry, it wasn't me!". A mistake or an inadvertent error. Put the whole thing to bed. But no ...another burden along with all the other layers. The week would end with an absence of recognition, gratitude or appreciation, of what I had sacrificed that week. Hard work from 4:30 a.m in the morning for six days. Sat lonely in the van for hours missing stimuli or conversation. Vacant.

A few weeks prior, Dad had acquired four jars of coffee, either from one of his wholesale customers or someone that knew someone. Tasked to take these back to the car across the yard at the bakery. Evident, once in my arms, appearing cumbersome but thought it okay. Half way there, struggling, my embarrassment obvious. A common event: I would get embarrassed by myself for myself. Ashamed by default. Embarrassed for being alive. Hating and self-loathing. Then it went. One of the jars dropped. Unplanned, unannounced, without reason or justification. Just did. Smash. Coffee and broken glass everywhere. Again, some spiritual matter consumed my being. Another cloak, another layer. Frozen in a spiritual attack of loathing, persecution, excruciating fear, guilt, and condemnation. Life and death.

"Idiot, can't you do anything right?" yelled my inner voice.

Pathetic. Complete and utter failure. Why do you bother? went the following thoughts.
Dad was duly informed on my return.

"Why didn't you sweep it up?" he said, as though the most common sense; obvious thing to do.

The event rendered a shuddering nervous wreck, traumatised.

We'd had the TB jab at school this year. My jab an iconic physical target for Josh. Almost like hitting bullseye. Punching on the spot daily, if not twice or thrice. Invariably, on the descent of the stairs or the ascent; cop a punch; a reminder of my position. Frequently bleed and heal, bleed and heal, as this ritual would ensue for months. Denied sympathy. Missing a defence or white-knight to be my Saviour.

Forbidden and prohibited from attending any teenage social gathering, party, school event, or the like. Not by parents, but Josh. Tantamount to torture. Imprisoned against one's will. Liberty and free social movement annulled. Captive. The consequences: violent, abusive, threatening, and sentenced to a future of persecution. A vacant post, to fight my corner, defend, an objector: step in and play judge. My response: unresponsive. Passive, pacifying, and ameliorative. Lacking a vindictive bone in my being, nor retort nor single vile word in defence. Void of slander circumventing retaliation. To accept my defeat and receive the outcome with acceptance. Of all Josh's retribution over the years, degrading outbursts, humiliations, physical attacks and the rest. I had nothing but love. Although everything that went on, justified. A Love like no other. Only God's Love.

1 Corinthians 13:4-8

"Love is patient and kind; Love does not envy or boast; it is not arrogant or rude. It does not insist on its own way; it is not irritable or resentful; it does not rejoice at wrongdoing, but rejoices with the truth. Love bears all things, believes all things, hopes all things, endures all things. Love never ends. As for prophecies, they will pass away; as for tongues, they will cease; as for knowledge, it will pass away."

Matthew 5:43-48

"You have heard that it was said, "You shall love your neighbour and hate your enemy." But I say to you, love your enemies and pray for those who persecute you, so that you may be sons of your Father who is in heaven. For he makes his sun rise on the evil and on the good, and sends rain on the just and on the unjust. For if you love those who love you, what reward do you have? Do not even the tax collectors do the same? And if you greet only your brothers, what more are you doing than others? Do not even the Gentiles do the same? You therefore must be perfect, as your heavenly Father is perfect."

John 15:9-17

"As the Father has loved me, so have I loved you. Abide in my love. If you keep my commandments, you will abide in my love, just as I have kept my Father's commandments and abide in his love. These things I have spoken to you, that my joy may be in you, and that your joy may be full. This is my commandment, that you Love one another as I have loved you. Greater love has no one than this, that someone lay down his life for his friends. You are my friends if you do what I command you. No longer do I call you servants, for the servant does not know what his master is doing; but I have called you friends, for all that I have heard from my Father I have made known to you. You did not choose me, but I chose you and appointed you that you should go and bear fruit and that your fruit should abide, so that whatever you ask the

Father in my name, he may give it to you. These things I command you, so that you will love one another."

The night of 6 March 1987, watching the news unfold on BBC. They didn't have "Breaking news" then, the Herald of Free Enterprise roll on roll off ferry capsized moments after leaving the Belgian port of Zeebrugge, killing 193 passengers and crew. It hit like a meteor. This is it then. Sixteen. Unknown to anyone, knowledge, personal traits, foibles, character, personality, or other. A vacuum of soul and self. I know it. God wish I didn't. Just me in this world. Incumbent to educate, acquire a job, provide financial security, and do it I must, void of alternatives. Who is going to support me? Come to my aid? Show mercy, grace, undeserved favour? Do it with unknown absent friends, family and support network. A personal one-one incomprehensible.

My starting place: the bi-weekly round of delivering the Gazette. Two thousand of the blighters. After school on a Thursday. It would necessitate several return trips, as just too many to take at once. In all weathers: dark, damp, wet, windy, cold, frost— the lot. But had a determination to get my tackle. To save, use my hard-earned money wisely. I'd want a house some day and obviously a pension.

The overwhelming desire to save oneself saw Jack excel in character. Denial of staple pleasures, social outlet, fun, enjoyment, materialism, shopping, happy-stuff and playing in the street with other kids. The world on his shoulders: a burden to self-sustain, independently alone, absence of impetus, chastisement, exhortation, or pastoral wisdom. The loneliness germinating; spending much of the day at school, lost in a world of his own. Arriving home to a vacant motel, twelve hours bi-weekly wandering the streets in the dark, delivering Gazettes alone.

The last day of school was a long walk home, particularly long. It wasn't the fact I was alone; a truism. But the last day of school, period. A truly momentous occasion. Literally, not just the last day of that year or that school, but the last day of my entire schooling life. Eclipsing childhood with scant responsibility to adulthood with the world on your shoulders. That beginning, all to be finalised on the way home. Just sat the last exam for what that was worth. Only half a mile distance. But for all intents and purposes, one hundred miles. The cumulative effect of the last three years aggregated into this day of finality. What did it all mean? What was it all for? More informed, equipped, skilled, educated to take on the world of work with life and social skills. Not a chance. Had it given me the tools, knowledge, and experience of team-work, problem-solving, contributing to a project. Resolutely obvious; an education negated. A positive negative. A minus one plus zero. Patently clearly uneducated with omission of basic skills. Last three years were lost, unidentified, missed, overlooked, and glossed over. Missing signing of books, hugs, goodbyes, tears or terms of endearment. The Eighties, but one of the most dystopian, dysfunctional, socially deprived schools in the country. An abyss of teachers, pupils, or secretary that would acknowledge my departure. An unknown ghostly figure that turned up for his mark. A silent witness.

Jack, obverse to puberty, girls, rebellion, or any other teenage attribute. In lock-down, bound in bondage. Void of feelings; period. Never mind feelings for girls. Seemingly bizarre to his outlook, what all the fuss about? Why are they so emotional and I unemotional? Must be the good guy if I don't kick-off as a rebel, become rude and possess hysterical emotion. He would develop unnaturally, socially, relationally, academically, emotionally, and spiritually. Stuck in time and in body; intransigent and immutable. Incapacitated of sensing the incredulous loneliness one would feel. A walking corpse. Alive in body but failing in spirit. Facial expression bland, passive, stoic, and inanimate.

From everything he had gleaned and weaned, observed and analysed, witnessed, experienced and self-taught. The negatives, impediments, obstacles, hindrances and opposition. Resulting as driven to the extreme. The desire to be 'Somebody', as opposed to an empty vessel. An inferred response to the melancholy, despair, oppression, and hopelessness. Yes I can. The seed sown in a bygone era would take root. The practical application and subsequent cultivation would ensue. Determined. Ambitious. Hard-working. Perseverance. Persistence. Risks. Fight.

An omission of discussion at home in terms of the next leg of life, whether to study and go to college or further education. Working-class. The appropriate objective: get a job straight away. A role of doctor, scientist, mathematician, or lawyer for someone else. A given point that a job was a job and the natural progression to go to Baxters, as Dad had.

Missing an immediate vacancy at Baxters. But as Mother would flannel the bakery director at the annual dinner and dance, mentioning her two son's now available and looking for work. It was coming. A family firm from inception whereby everyone knew everyone, had been there donkeys years. Probably known of as 'Tots' from the company's employee population. But now grown up. Well, sixteen. Ready to enter the world of work. Continuing as stand-in van-lads, unofficially. Cash in hand: albeit five pounds for nine hours work. Noting willingness, commitment and ability to regularly rise at 4:30 a.m daily. Hard-working and enthusiastic. Dad had set a good reputation for our family name. An exemplary record of punctuality and continuous service; missing absenteeism. Walking to work in the snow; cold or flu. Proud, responsible, with integrity. After several weeks on different rounds persevering and faithful, sooner or later it would translate into being fully employed. Retaining our first real job. And so it did.

Jack had developed an ability to self-punish intrinsically on demand. The fear and urgency of lateness inconceivable. Immaculate in presentation. Unblemished smock, highly polished shoes: a daily ritual, regime. Well groomed and pruned. Avoiding any criticism or disparaging remarks at any cost. A perfectionist attitude. The contemporary colleagues would find him odd. Anti-social, avoiding any social contact: withdrawn and introverted. Often came back to him that fellow van-lads thought him 'strange'. Exemplary attendance and laudable punctuality. Even through health problems, enduring suffering and soldiering on. The right thing to do. As gleaning and environment suggested. Inconceivable to remain passive in role or status. Had an agenda, plan of action. Unthinkable to do the same thing as his Dad. Desirable advancement, promotion, responsibility, and achievement. The first milestone: to gain respect, credibility, and demonstrable trustworthiness. Pass the driving test, drive, retain own round, then see where things take him.

The director Mother had coerced into giving us a job had since retired. His successor incomparable in character: morals, loyalty, age, education, and social background. Poles apart. The new guy, Eric, apparently a Quaker, had an exceptional education behind him, most likely private school. At twenty-eight had been appointed to director seniority. Ruthless in his endeavour to succeed and excel. His management style autocratic and dogmatic. The word would get around of what he'd done and intentions. Fear resonated around the firm. Sacking colleagues on a whim. An unknown crevice in the company he couldn't influence: change, adapt or shut down. Yielding power and control right up to Mr. Baxter. He would dispose of the company cat. Any casual labour that was trying to make a few quid to top up their dole money refused immediately. Those with learning difficulties or social impediments, opting for a stand-in van-lad position to retain some dignity and have a pint at the weekend, stopped in their tracks.

On arrival back at the firm from a typical day with Bryan. Summoned to Eric's office by the supervisor, Mr. P. Mixed feelings. Excitement fused with fear and anxiety. Am I getting a promotion? What does he want me for? What did I do wrong? Haven't been late or spoken to anyone, only done my job to the best of my ability. Seemingly odd as I entered. Mr. P present also, suggestive. The door closed and the three of us sat in this impending meeting. The agenda unknown. All the hallmarks of something witnessed on TV. A questioning, detective, inquisition-type scenario. Unappearing, the occasion presented for them to praise or recognise for outstanding hard work, diligence, punctuality, and integrity.

"It has been brought to my attention that you have been spreading rumours about the supervisor's fiddling." said Eric in his opening line.

Shock, horror: "What the..."

Literally in shock. Breathing adapted to shortened rapid breaths: facial colour bright red. Panic-stricken. A bizarre moment. Awareness that they knew I was struggling, stuttering, stammering, to express myself. Attempting to extricate from something innocent. Having figured out what was going on in my head, Mr P sat at the side of me knowing what I know. Convicted there and then. And for the moment was about to say
"Yes, that's right!"

But sense of righteousness: self-imposed judicial legality would come to bear and quell any lie implicated, guilty or complicit in any way.

"Sorry, I don't know what you are talking about!" renounced convincingly.
"I don't talk to anyone. Actually known as the 'quiet one' that's unspoken.
How could I possibly spread rumours to whom?"
"But surely you speak to your dad and brothers when you go home?" he would prosecute.

That was a bizarre scenario anyway, knowingly disengaged and we sit in silence for most meal times. But that's something else.

"Yes, like normal families, we share and exchange how our day has gone and discuss accordingly. But the idea we discuss supervisor's fiddling is poppycock, frankly!"

"Tell me right now what you know or walk out of that door and never return!" he expressed resolutely and steadfastly.

Stuck to my guns.

"Sorry but I can't tell what is unknown. You'll have to do that because I don't know anything."

Having invested so much time, effort, energy, and good-will into my job, this is how I'm compensated. Devastated. My mind's eye hadn't seen beyond working here. Unthinkable to imagine what the future held without Baxters. A dearth of skills, qualifications, abilities or positive experiences could be conveyed to some future employer. Allowed to leave the room. Confused and perplexed. Bewildered by what the previous twenty minutes had done to the atmosphere and spiritual environment. Things would never be the same again after this. Uncertain whether returning to work the following day or not. Things just got left. Distraught, tearful, and dejected. Making my way through the bakery, to the yard where Bryan waiting in the queue for the van wash. I entered the cab and burst into tears.

"What's up?" he enquired.
Almost as gutted as me by the expression and concern on his face.
In the midst of crying and breathing erratically my words would 'blubble' out indiscriminately.

"They want to sack me!"
"What?"
"Yes, they want to sack me!"
"They said, Tell us what you know or you're out of that door!"
"Word for word."
"Apparently spreading rumours about the supervisors' fiddling."
A look of disbelief shot across his face.

"They duped me into it. Union representatives absent. Surreptitiously stitched me up."

Bryan expressed his sorrow, disappointment, and said, "Sorry kid!"

After twelve months of working with vacant holiday, days off or break in service, our seventeenth birthday looming. Mum and Dad had gone away for the week and left us at home. Regularly going to bed in the afternoon after an early start. During the nap, on the day of our birthday: a knock at the door. Only the bloody driving instructor.

"You've been booked onto your first driving lesson," shouted the instructor from outside the house.

Josh went first then he came back for me. Still bleary-eyed, half asleep, perplexed, and shocked at the spectacle. The instructor pissed me off after a while. Arriving up ten minutes late and dropping us off ten minutes early. Apparently giving him time to travel to his next client. A contentious start. Becoming a consummate observer. An idiot could be identified at a thousand yards. The learner car—a mini, the old type—we drove. Sat in close proximity. A prerequisite to do an emergency stop. But given my track record in terms of paradoxically refraining and restraining. An attempt to not kill the imaginary child but to stop the tyres skidding, or the passenger and driver lunging forward and subsequently smashing our heads on the windscreen. The brakes hit upon the given signal by the instructor. My innate insecurities did exactly that. Not to screech the tyres or jerk us forward. The brake suppressed moderately hard. But not hard enough. We must have travelled a few yards further; slowly arriving to a halt. The instructor indignant with rage. His face boiling, red in colour.

"What the hell was that? You would have killed a child right there. What were you thinking?"

Devastating. Criticism and negative words were disagreeable with me.

"Have another go!" he affirmed, impatiently.

The routine repeated several times. On the cusp of getting the signal to STOP!, the brakes were hit, but mildly, moderately, not as though a child was in front of the car. An attempt to pre-empt and perfect an error before it had occurred. Self-preservation. He went absolutely berserk. His face enraged, despair enveloped him. Shot out of his side of the car like a bullet out of a gun. Raced round to my side, flung the door open, screamed at me: "Get out!" Ranting and raving all the while. Sheepishly and nervously entering the passenger's side knowing I'd be shown up. He'd demonstrate how to do it properly.

A few months later when the accident occurred. Innocent. The guy behind. While waiting at a junction for a break in traffic, shunted from behind. Usually shafted from above but this time from the rear. A shock: my first incident with another driver and the jolt itself. As it happened, something and nothing, a minor dent but significant enough to warrant repairs at the garage through insurance. Impatient and desperate to get home as fast as possible to inform of my experience. To be reassured and relieve the distress and talk it all out what had occurred. On arrival home my heart pulsating anxiously. Eager and longing to share. It appeared Mum and Dad were out. Only Josh and Paul sat in watching TV.

"I've just been rear-ended, shunted from behind!" said in a hurried, desperate, anxious voice.
Silent.
"I've just been rear-ended, shunted from behind!" repeated, breathing heavily.
Still silent.
Indifferent to look up, or flinch. Failing to come out to look at the car or ask if I was okay.

I had become an accomplished angler. Self-taught from the beginning. The four annual matches at Baxters were my primary focus out of work. Diligently serious about my sport to the point of doing a recce to check the venue, conditions, habitat, and best baits to use. My performance remarkable given, but a teenager missing formal tuition or instruction. The weights respectable, up against grown men in their forties who'd been at it for years. An unknown phenomenon but my stellar performance rendered the winner. Dad would go along too. But more out of duty than anything else. Unenthusiastic and unmotivated. Another disturbing event. Dad unspoken the whole day. I think it does something to somebody in their head when a common natural human act fails. More so when someone is so biologically and intimately related to you. The absence of connection, silence of engagement, and omission of communication. Theoretically intimately related. Dad wasn't intimate by any stretch of the imagination. On the contrary. But having succeeded and achieved my inward goal, the ultimate prize of winning my first fishing match. My destiny and pinnacle of achievement. I had arrived in my world. But met with great sadness, disappointment, and dejection. Unrecognised and uncommented to note this joyous, jubilant, triumphant moment. Void.

While walking up the bank weighing in, from peg to peg, I could hear voices of the other competitors. Viewing the weight record sheet, attempting to ascertain who had caught the heaviest weight.

"Old Fred's lad's done well! He could well be in the top three!" noted one of the other anglers.

My heart almost had a fit. A bolt out of the blue: name mentioned: well not quite. Fred's lad will do for me, for now. A shot of adrenaline burst through my body, euphoric, excited, pulse racing, alive. A stark moment. It fitted in with everything known, suspected, gleaned weaned, observed, and intuition loaned. The absence of being known, acknowledged or spoken to would have a profound effect when acknowledged, name mentioned or discourse entered into. The analogy to a patient being resuscitated by de-fibrillation. To be seen would enliven, re-ignite: allowed to feel alive momentarily. Although downsides to this. Protracted perennial periods of invisibility. Though longing for this ideal. Also my nemesis. The shame that lived within, guilt, badness, self-loathing and corruption. An obverse effect. Bright red. Ashamed. Fearful of attack. Can't cope. Must escape, avoid, and evade the situation. Socially inept and incapacitated. Empty of social norms to conjure up from historical experiences or nuances acquired over my childhood. An untenable inability to deal with attention of any kind. A prescient dichotomous perennial trait.

Over the last twelve months my dedication had amassed several accolades. Fisherman of the year, winner of my group, and winner of the match. A company annual fishing presentation evening had been organised. The event whereby a presentation was made in front of the two hundred employees. Held in a banquet centre with a meal, music, and drinks. Probably the most significant time of my life; surreal. An alien experience. How would I deal with all those people looking at me? What would I say if they wanted a speech?

As the weekend of the presentation evening approached my giddiness, inner excitement, and hopeful expectation took centre stage. Silently counting the days down in my head for this momentous occasion. An event per se, for me to be driving. Mum, Dad, and their friends, a bit of a chauffeur experience. Passing the driving test weeks prior, so all relatively new. But enjoyed the grown-up experience of driving own car with passengers. Josh had passed first time, and to say we started lessons on the same day; didn't bode well requiring two more attempts. Unhelpful the instructor allocated, in fear of error, inadvertent mistakes or misunderstanding. Notwithstanding the day of the test itself.

The pressure and responsibility to equal Josh. Compounded in an already stressed, anxious, self-conscious, doubting vulnerable person. Had failed twice in the instructor's car and disliked him anyway. Took it upon myself to drive own car, which was much more at ease in. Passed third time.

I'd got us there at the reception of the presentation hall on time. December, and had forecast snow. A rural venue in the Peak District, high on the Pennines. Bryan, Mum, Dad, Dad's colleagues, other fishermen, and Mr P were all in attendance. Oh, and that awful man Joe had turned up with his minions. The emotional pain he'd inflicted still raw. Why did he have to turn up? Pacifying and ameliorative, alien to be vindictive, retaliate, or seek retribution. Although justified. Unbecoming to seek vengeance in terms of how I felt about Joe, maintaining a righteous, morally correct code. But this was a chance for the spiritual powers to play their hand. Of all the vitriolic, cruel, churlish, callous words that have left your mouth. You are now going to be forced to sit in an audience without escape and endure my moment of glory. This talented young man: fatherless, orphaned, self-taught in every discipline, degenerated, and disparaged, whom you have berated and degraded, and compounded existing humiliations. He is now going to be honoured and will receive all the trophies awarded this night in front of your very eyes. My mood one of ebullience, proud for an unprecedented occasion.

Impossible to hold all the trophies. The fisherman of the year, huge. A helping hand required to return them back to the table. Upon walking back, visualising Mum and Dad's beaming smile, proud of me. Delighted of my achievement, euphoric, clapping with the rest of the attendees. Redundant. Missing eye contact, unspoken.

Three years prior we'd opted away from the touring caravan towards a static. Juxtaposed to the River Trent, a lake across the road and another Carp pond fifty yards in the other direction. What more could one want? Dad knew someone at work that had organised a fishing match on the Trent only a few miles away. Suggested I might like to partake. Without a doubt, I'm in. The day of the match arrived and my behaviour was typical of a pending match. Giddy, excited, expectant, and hopeful. Very competitive despite being marred, undermined, and ailing. Couldn't believe my luck or skill when hooked on to what perceived to be an almighty fish. A very respectable two-pound-ish perch. My zeal and thoughts would get ahead of me. This is it! In the bag, literally. Hope jumped up, giddiness went ballistic, almost feeling good about myself. Mum and Dad invariably unsupportive or stood side-by-side in solidarity. A pillar of support merely by attendance. Wasn't like that. Watching for ten minutes. What more did I want?

"But we're getting fed up now. The dog needs walking." they would recite.
They had turned up with the dog to do their bit.
"How's it going?" asked Dad.
"Good..., done really well and caught a massive perch," ebullient with pride.
"Thinking I'm in for a good chance of winning it!" said with hopeful expectation.
"Oh no, don't think so. I wouldn't build your hopes up," he replied.

Within minutes they had gone. Left to finish the other three hours alone. The match ended and time for weigh-in. Despite Dad ruining my day and destroying the whole experience, still a glimmer of hope and anticipation in my belly. The anxious momentum would grow as nearing the final outcome. Noting other competitors' weight, comparing against mine instantaneously in my head. Then it came. A bitter-sweet moment. I'd done it. The perch tipped the scales for me literally. Won outright. Meaningless. Gutted and devastated. Languishing in sorrow and sadness. Appearing satisfied and thankful outwardly but overwhelmingly disappointed internally. Didn't matter how hard I tried, focused, or persevered. A vacuum of approval, praise, recognition or acknowledgement.

A typical weekend at the caravan, characterised as Dad sleeping or up Mother's cuff. I'd be fishing alone, Paul lounging about, Josh gone off with some girl or gone fishing elsewhere on his own. On an evening visiting a local pub with their friends on the site. Invariably unattended. The social phenomena of pub, unfamiliar people, Mother speaking for and on behalf; excluded from conversation. Unalluring. Differing with my years of conditioning: also withdrawn and anti-social. Therefore, a perpetual cycle of social fear, anxiety, withdrawn, low self-esteem, and insecurity. The rare occasion I'd dare to go: met with great sadness. Unable to speak, feeling imprisoned: missing the keys. But having keys would I be able to unlock the door? Trapped. My intuition knew it. Incongruous. Someday the real Jack would stand up. Rising up like a phoenix. A vision of a sunrise but somehow translated to 'Son, Rise' in my mind. But this most certainly wasn't the real Jack. Bound, captive, shackled and under a yoke of Sin.

Driving my own car down to the site and back home alone. Fishing for five hours alone, then an evening watching TV in the caravan, for another week at work speaking the odd one-word reply on-demand. This is how my seventeenth year, approaching eighteen, would play out. The anticipation of the eighteenth looming. It wasn't so much we'd be officially adults but allowed to drive the seven-and-a-half tonne vans at work. The role of 'driver'. The self-imposed discipline extraordinary for the age. The level of self-control applied, at will; prolific. Regimented. Views contrary to the average youth. Staying in and saving money. The goal: buy a car in the near future. A highly moralistic rigid legal framework from which to live one's life. Also, under age didn't align itself with my outlook on submitting to the law. The drinking age is eighteen, therefore will wait patiently until that threshold is reached. The proverbial mocking, criticising, and making fun of my esoteric views from my peers. But more than that, underlying conflicts and dysfunctions within my soul. Spiritually, mentally, and emotionally. The experience of being in a social environment would compel me to leave and never return. A recluse, hidden and withdrawn. Unable to form a connection: alien. The paranoia, self-conscious inadequacy, socially inept, bound, self-loathing born out of frustration, anger, and hatred. Safe if alone. All those experiences could be avoided. Therefore, staying in every work night and every weekend.

The eighteenth would arrive unobtrusively: seamlessly, a normal working day. Parents away, unknown relatives in sight, and brothers absent. The usual impersonal dutifully contrived birthday card. A negligible connection to the recipient. However, negating the personal euphoria of an eighteenth birthday one might experience. My focus more aligned with promotion, driving the van, and getting my own round. Earning a respectable salary to get the car and a step closer to independence. Missing a single dependent. Either make or break it, sink or swim. The previous two years working hard diligently, wearing tie, clean ironed smock, gleaming black polished shoes with an almost glossy and chrome finish. Smart, punctual, polite, helpful, and agreeable. Available, enthusiastic and self motivated. Just a case of time. In the right place at the right time. It was coming. They'd have to. Beyond reasonable doubt.

Sure enough, it did. My driver, Bryan, had done his back in lifting a bucket of water to wash the car. He'd be off work for six weeks. An opportunity. As I had worked on the round for the last two years, I knew the difficult customers: where to be at what time, daily routines, and quantities of bread. A natural logical decision to take to the helm. Notwithstanding recently passing the age of eighteen, which would qualify for insurance. Game on. Traits of my character presented a dis-service. The desire for responsibility and seniority. As much allure fused with 'OMG!' What have you done now? Fear, doubt, worry, and anxiety. The main one: how would I calculate the invoice to the customer? Maths were less than dire, an inadequate education. The obvious solution to ask Dad. He'd been doing the job for over twenty years. Surely, a 'No-brainer'.

"Dad, can you show me how to do the bills at work?"
"Errr.... Go and have a look at a ready-reckoner!" came the reply.

That was it. Something else to figure out alone. Wikipedia or Google non-existent in the Eighties. It never crossed my mind either, how socially inept, introverted, and hidden. All I know, normal. But only when thrown in the deep end or immersed in a social situation the anxiety would bolt. That said, my strength of character would see me through. Failing to hinder but carrying on regardless. I'll deal with it.

A behavioural cultural pattern existed within the fabric at Baxters. One of fraud. In an unorthodox sense but nonetheless still an iniquity. As well as drivers, supervisors were at it too. Surreptitiously releasing quantities of bread through the check-out, but electing not to make any record of it. Therefore, allowing the driver to sell the goods to his customers retaining the profit. Joe had been the consummate pilferer, not only from the bakery but also the customers, and if that was insufficient, siphoning diesel from the company van to his car. Informing me to take a tray of bread in the shop with an empty tray underneath, charging the customer for two. Expecting me to deal with the fallout, contentious customer. While he would hide at the rear of the van like a coward.

Of all my quirks, foibles, and idiosyncrasies, the observational trait exemplary. The supervisor, Mr P, asked me on this particular day to take a rack of bread and leave it at the back of Mr. X's van. Was I the most innocent, trusted, perceived less risky option? Quiet, unseen, less likely to tell anyone. I knew what was happening. Thesc two had been friends for years. Had grown up together, went fishing, and played golf. Retaining the new found knowledge. Registering a mental note. Several other examples of father supervisor, son driver relationships existed. Certain friends of friends. The drivers that would deliver to Baxters' proprietary shops also at it. They would pilfer and do a deal with the wholesale drivers, both making on the deal.

Post six weeks managing the round with my own van-lad. Bryan was returning to work and had proven my worth. A commendable six weeks. No complaints. Excellent punctuality and great service. Exemplary. Now capable and demonstrable experience. They'd put me on the hardest more gruelling routes; as a relative youth. What only the young had the energy to perform due to the demanding nature of the job. Start at three in the morning. Twenty racks of bread to drag out of the bakery yourself. Haul it into the back of the van. Three drop-off-points, Newark, Grantham, and Stamford. Then the return journey home. Frequently nodding off at the wheel, driving in the dark: whirring of the engine and heater on full blast. Dangerous especially at sixty mph. Communicating this to Mr P, but unsympathetic: told to go and have an hour's sleep then come back to work in the afternoon. After a while they had moved me onto my own round. Delivering around Doncaster. Missing a van-lad with this one. All alone. Up at three again. Twenty racks, off to Sainsbury's to unload one tray at a time. A struggle, often sweating, panicking, not coping, worrying, paranoid, despairing at times. Regularly forgetting the French sticks, or teacakes requiring a turn around, costing more time. The urgency and fear of lateness wholly unhelpful. An irrational but authentic phobia. Even on the motorway cruising the middle lane, foot to the floor, overtaking, thinking I'll arrive at my destination quicker. To realise just passing the junction should have got off at. Making things progressively worse. I'd have to drive on to the next junction, go around the round-about come back down the other side, get off then make the junction should have got off in the first place. Wasting another thirty minutes. My heart in constant distress Always, racing, panicking, palpitations. An obvious inability to cope. But my strict moral code would supersede any failure or regressive steps. During sleep there'd be dreams of:

"Had I ordered this, done that? Forget to do the other?"

Even while at work, thoughts would cross my mind in a mad panic thinking some awful calamity is about to occur. Like I've forgotten the scones for Gateway.

At this point an unfortunate accident occurred at home. Trapping my finger in the circular ring that opens the cupboard door. It must have been fractured. Bent at the joint nearest my finger nail. Attended triage at the local hospital. They had put a splint on and requested I return for an appointment for a scan to see the damage. Relaying this information to Mr P. Imperative that I attend for this appointment. Therefore, requiring the day off work. An atmosphere of resistance; impervious. My observations were they were opposed and objectionable. In fact, intransigent. Informed I should call Mr P that afternoon to resolve the dispute.

A dearth of phone calls in my life. Who would call me? Missing a motive, prior, to call anyone. Uninformed and untrained of how to use a telephone or what to say: the telephone etiquette. Another anxious moment. Should I really have to discuss the merits of a hospital appointment when my finger is practically broken? Is it really up for discussion? My dignity feeling threatened. Ahead of the final outcome. The phone rang, and Mr P answered. The information related to him.

"My finger is practically broken, they have arranged an appointment for a specialist to scan and examine to determine any further treatment, I need the day off!" I pleaded.

"That's not going to happen!"
"What?"
"No, take that day off and you won't come back to your existing job!" he asserted.
"What the...?"

Never did go to that appointment. Carrying on as normal. Working, driving and writing invoices with my partially broken index finger.

A month later the driving accident occurred. The fog exceptionally dense all over Yorkshire. The distance of visibility from my cab window about twenty yards. A treacherous morning and hyper-vigilance indicator several points higher than normal. Desperate to arrive at the next drop-off point promptly. Fully aware the driving speed was too fast. Forty mph at twenty-yards visibility didn't equate. But the urgency and desire to quell the feeling of badness by lateness, the speed I drove would take precedence. The immediate focal point blank. Alertness primed to optimum, recording the slightest sign of movement ahead. Insufficient. The woman driver's fog lights were off. Out of nowhere a long line of standing traffic presented itself. A split second for the acknowledgement and identification to reach my brain. Heart missing a beat. The van ten feet away when I hit the anchors. Too late. Swerved into the opposite side of the road where oncoming traffic would travel to avoid full impact to the rear of the first car. Too late. Had literally ploughed into the rear-end smashing on impact side windows and destroying the whole back-end, near-side of the car. She was hysterical. Obviously we'd have to exchange details. Accepting full responsibility and so overwhelmingly apologetic. Berating self for stupidity. Common sense. What were you thinking? No bread delivery is more important than causing a serious accident. The fellow male drivers would step out of their cars to discover the commotion. Angry and expressing displeasure. I was eighteen.

Fortunately, the big heavy-weight 7.5 tonne truck with little sign of significant damage. Still drivable. Noticeable it had been in an accident, but not to the point of being un-roadworthy. The woman's car written off. Able to get back in the van and carry on with the round. Despite shock, trembling and shaking. Unable to shift my thoughts to anything else. Going over and over in my mind. Will I get thc sack? What will they say back at the firm? How will I tell them? The day would proceed, deliveries met and would return to the firm as though a normal day. On arrival into the office, my chosen method of submission and tentative delivery of information was one of subtlety.

"Are there any insurance claim forms knocking about anywhere by any chance?"
"Why would you want one of those, Jack?" said the supervisor at hand.
"Errr... I kind of had a little accident."
"Oh right... what kind of accident?"
"Eerrrr ...well, I kind of ploughed into the back of a line of standing traffic writing off the car nearest."

"What condition is the van in?" the supervisor questioned.

My heart sank, devastated. What condition is the van in? Is he for real?
What with the fractured finger débâcle and now this. Any self respect I might have once possessed was slowly waning and deprecating. Compounded by an already annulled self-esteem and inadequacy.

Impatient to get home to tell someone. Although having so much experience of being unheard, misunderstood, and unsympathetic. Expectations were cynical. Were they also going to dumb it down and dismiss? Make light, or just walk away. Informing Dad.

"Oh, right!"

End of.

I told Mum what they had said at work and how wrong that was. Doesn't anyone care about how I am or how I feel?

"What did they say that for?" she questioned, with her valuable input.

The probationary period on the Doncaster journey would prove satisfactory. Vacant blunders, or cock-ups. Only the ones I knew about. The week prior to Christmas week, my orders were exceedingly beyond what the van was able to carry, even on several trips back and forth. An unforeseen scenario until the morning of the event. But resulted in a request being made to Mr. P that I was overloaded and needed a hand to get all the stock to Sainsbury's. One of his minions available that week to do such a task. Noted he'd take four racks of bread on my behalf: nine hundred and sixty loaves. On arrival at the store, having all my bread checked, the store checker brought it to my attention that one hundred loaves were short. Immediately evident what had happened. Stitched up again.

"Okay!" I said.
"I'll make it right with you in the morning."

Thinking I'll have words on my return to the firm. Tell Mr P I'm not happy. His mate has done Sainsbury's out of one hundred loaves and I'm neither taking the can for it nor losing that money. Mr P wasn't having any of it. Dismissive.

"Well, you'll have to sort it out with them in the morning!"

Unconcerned of the intention to convey without stipulating explicitly. Your mate has robbed Sainsbury's and left me in the shit, to foot the bill. I chose my words carefully and succinctly not to antagonise or aggravate by making false allegations:

"Andy dropped that bread off and they are saying they are short!" said assertively.
"It's not my problem. He dropped it off, you'll have to sort it out with him." he replied dismissively.

Knowing the score—unlikely to admit his mate had made some easy Christmas money under his nose and on his watch. Moreover, he knew I knew too.

The next morning, bricking myself, knowing a no-win situation. Andy, a notorious hard nut akin to Vinnie Jones. A violent past, belligerent, and scheming. Exhibiting physical abilities readily to unsuspecting van-lads. Twisting fingers, punching at will. Making threats. Wasn't someone you challenged if you cherished life. Mr. P antagonistic. I'd have to be covert but brash. All the bread had been offloaded. The stress and anxiety kicking in the closer the checker came to aggregating today's delivery plus the missing one hundred loaves from yesterday. Just waiting for the inevitable. Then disbelief.

"Oh yes, I've seen them. That's everything!"

Couldn't believe it. I'd got away with it. A huge relief and a weight lifted off my shoulders.

A decision made to alter my given route and elect as 'spare driver'. One who would stand-in for the driver in question, on leave. A different journey each week. My first journey to Nottingham. Primed by the driver the week preceding. What to expect, times, places, tools of the job. But then noted in a wink-wink, nudge-nudge fashion. Upon arrival at Sainsbury's, leave two trays of bread on the van.

"Oh right!" I said. Knowing exactly, surreptitiously inducted into this practice unwittingly. An unspoken agreement. A nod and a wink. You know how to play it.

Caught red-handed. Discovered instantaneously not by a blue-collar worker but Manager of the Store.

"I'm two trays short here!"
"Oh right ... are you sure?"
"Yes, I've double-checked, definitely two trays short."

Shit, we've been rumbled.
"Oh okay! Let me see if we've missed anything."
"Ah yes, there they are right at the back!"

I thought we'd got away with it. Upon arrival back at the firm, waiting. Summoned to the office. Presented the sequence of events and told: "You're fired!"

THE EIGHTIES

My first experience of unemployment. A purposeless existence. Unqualified, inexperienced, lacking in skills, anti-social, poor communicator, and zero confidence. Unyielding support, either from the government, family, friends, or charitable organisations. Merely, me, myself, and I. A CV an unknown entity; letter-writing unfamiliar. Unavailable word processors in the Eighties, not in the wider public domain. The jobseeker's allowance a meagre, paltry allowance. Enough to pay Mum board and survive: nothing more. Void of financial hand-outs, support from so-called 'loved ones'. Unsure which way to turn. Annulled of positive endorsements, abilities, traits, or attributes to define in a particular vocation. For instance, academic, care, construction, builder, service, catering etc. A blank slate. Transparent at that. Out of desperation jumping at anything and everything to secure 'The job'. A protracted period of frustration, poverty of spirit, social, financial, and mental. The historical environment unfavourable. Residing in a socially deprived area, poor literacy rates, educational attainment, underperforming school, dysfunctional family, unloved, friendless: enemies plentiful. A county with its industrial and economic heritage torn apart. Redundancies and unemployment at record levels. Coal pits closing; communities rendered incapacitated. Steel manufacturing would migrate to the Far East or Eastern Europe.

The best I could do: warehouse, packing, order-picking, maybe a bakery or food processing plant. At least my credentials would elucidate working with food, managing orders, handling cash, driving and had accomplished three years' excellent service; unblemished. Notwithstanding the tumultuous departure which will go unmentioned. Missing excursions, holidays, weekends away, shopping trips, drinks, visits, or anything construed leisurely or pleasurable. Relatives absent: only biologically related. Left to it: sink or swim. Unsympathetic. Mum, Dad, Josh, and Paul failing to acknowledge my plight. Too consumed in their own world to bother. Spending two Christmase's, New Year's eves, and birthdays alone. Friday nights sat in watching TV. Weekends lost, troubled, lonely, and helpless.

Josh would go on his first holiday without parents. Inevitably, excluded and uninvited. Opting to go with the two acquaintances we both grew up with; now commandeered as 'his' friends.

More than twelve long months had elapsed before anything tangible would present itself. Then in the local press, an advert for a relatively local dairy processing plant, producing yoghurt for major supermarkets. A temporary position generating a few quid would pay for some well-deserved trainers, go towards the insurance on the car and maybe even enjoy myself with the proceeds. Another terrifying experience. Entering an unknown social situation, void of inkling in terms of tasks, responsibilities, and duties. Untrained and feeling inadequate. Working in a fridge all day. Literally. A one-hour break for lunch, and that was it. Six while two. Four women in the warm side of the factory packing yoghurts into boxes of four, aided by automated machinery. They'd have a fifteen-minute break every hour and rotate between them. Failing to get taken off: in the fridge all day. Lifting crates onto a conveyor belt then the four-packs from the other side to be stacked up and distributed to their destination. A stereotypical workforce from South Yorkshire, originating from former mining communities: uneducated, antisocial, rude, tribal, belligerent, with colloquial vernacular. Assigned to a guy with several years' service: confident showing me around and informing tasks and duties. Attaching to him as security, safety, and guidance. A transitory period before the senses alerted upon observation; attempting to shake me off. Unsightly to his peers or tribal credibility to have some 'newbie' tagging along, seeking to befriend him. Had to maintain the hard-man image. Vacant of social etiquette. Failing to enquire or acknowledge me. Within a short period to assess the situation; patently clear. Now shown around; on my own. The following week on arrival at the canteen for breakfast, palpitations, anxiety, and worry would pervade. Exceptionally busy, a dearth of places to sit. Hoping by the time I get served someone will have vacated, therefore able to eat my breakfast in peace. A frenetic atmosphere, people, jostling in and out, queuing, shouting, and talking: a real mélee. On making payment for my breakfast several recce's across the room had been conducted. Identifying a vacant seat with three other guys. That one will do. On arrival my tray lowered onto the table. About to take my seat when the guy next said:

"Can't sit there pal!"
"Uh!"
"No, that seat's taken!"
"No it's not I'm about to take it."
"No you can't. It's my mate's, who's in the queue." he remonstrated.

Allowed to stand missing a seat for fifteen minutes, all the while breakfast going cold. It epitomised the level of ignorance, standard of education, and tribal community I had got involved in. Rarely called by name the whole time employed. They had identified similarities between me and a son of one of the directors. Therefore, addressed by this guy's name for the duration. After accounting for the difficult working conditions, contentious attitudes, name-calling, and general level of dis-respect, enough was enough. Unworthy of a resignation letter or phone call. The best method of communicating my dis-satisfaction to walk out and never return.

Back to the drawing board. Returning to the dole. Although a whisper a small local bakery, Jewitts, could potentially take someone on. Notorious for taking Baxters' rejects. Several of my former colleagues had ended up there; seemingly an appropriate salvage opportunity. The manager, Phillip: appearing an angry, menacing man. Had already expressed on the phone about his dad dying. Excusing himself from the lack of communication and failure to keep updated on developments. But desperate and needed the money. The job would entail starting at five in the morning similar to Baxters. Delivering their baked produce to local stores within a fifty-mile radius. As the journey and addresses of delivery points were unfamiliar, we would work as a duo. He had the company car and for me to drive the seven-and-a-half tonne van. The van unfamiliar too. The gear stick in an odd position, controls appearing cumbersome and unnatural. Dark and missing interior lights revealing the controls. Within minutes he had lost his temper, fuming with anger.

"Get out!
Useless!"
"Let me do it!"
"Go! You take the car, I'll drive this!"

A good move, driving the car in luxury. He would set off first knowing the destination, for me to follow. Setting off at a pace more akin to a racing driver. Challenging to keep up. It crossed my mind, what if he ever went out of sight or through lights, leaving me waiting there at red? A very stressful first few hours merely trying to keep up never mind understand the job at hand. We had travelled as far as Leeds to a major store, then to return more locally. Nearing 8:00 a.m, the rush hour and school run. Traffic was horrendous. His erratic, speeding driving unabated. Then in an instant, lost him. Out of sight. Where did he go? Turn off or straight on? Can't see him anywhere. Non-existent mobile phones, the Eighties. Shit! What a plonker, I thought. Him, not me.

Beginning to visualise the impending meet-up and reconciliation. But what of his reaction. Sufficient evidence gleaned in my mind that would be unpleasant. Irate at best: mad or angry, probably. The more time elapsed, more anxious and desperate I would feel. Knowing each minute passed, another minute later to our customers. Self inflicted. His own stupid fault and actions. Has to take full responsibility for that. A long line of standing traffic on the approach to a large round-about. My car positioned about fifteenth in line. For a split second scarcely glanced in the near-side mirror. A mad man bolting down the road. Bright red, panting, like the house was on fire. Only bloody Phillip. Didn't feel good on his approach. Commencing with a kick. Synonymous to a mad rabid dog. A violent senseless man enraged. As though his entire life's problems had amassed into this very moment. Had culminated and aggregated to the ultimate precipice of explosive rage. Yanked and flung my door wide open. Felt like a scene out of a film. Based on the drama alone, surreal. In slow motion.

"What the f*****hell do you think you are doing?"
Kicks the door.
"You f*** ing idiot!"
Kicks the door again.
"Where did you f****ing go?"

He stormed off, shouting, swearing, cursing on his way. Traumatised, shaking and trembling for the rest of the day. Exhausting exposed to a vitriolic oppressive environment. That was it. Unthinkable to go back for another day. Tantamount to abuse. Granted, something I had grown up with and very well accustomed to but a line had been crossed. No job or amount of money is worth being treated in that way. Failing to compensate for that day. In vain.

Apparent innocuous signs all was unwell with my soul. On driving to the caravan, a day with Mum and Dad that's all I had. On my return anger would rise up within, unwittingly. The unquantifiable metric of loneliness, isolation, and alienation. The past. My demons. Rage erupted in a spirit of fire, uncontrollable. However, the intrinsic ability to override senses, the innate instantaneous ability to suppress and deny emotion or feeling, honed to a high calibre. Shoving it down once again. Play a music tape similar to Bridget Jones Diary, in the car 'All by myself.' But how sad. Often manifested by driving. Foot to the floor on the accelerator. Wheel spinning and screeching. Speeding without thought or care.

Post-three months of the last débâcle, brought to my attention of a 'Job Club'. Attendance is five days per week from nine in the morning till twelve lunch-time. The goal was to write as many hand-written letters as possible within this time frame, speculatively to local employers. To my amazement a lone letter would succeed in its intended purpose by securing the ultimate prize. An interview. The exercise hadn't been as futile as first perceived. There was life out there. The position: a milk man. Six days per week. Up at three in the morning for a thirty-minute drive to the depot. Again, the general depot population of all male would typify my former experiences of male-dominated working-class environments. Abrupt, abrasive, berating, critical, mocking, and distant. They soon clocked on; hard-working, punctual, young, athletic, and strong. As soon as the initial induction training completed; onto taking a round for the week while the resident milk man on holiday. The fear of failure and approval seeking would eclipse a harmonious, peaceful, moderated approach to work. The art of over exerting oneself, punishing, over-zealous, rigorous in attitude, and sentiment was second nature. The fellow colleagues referring as 'Kwik-fit', returning to the depot quicker than the regular man. Literally racing around, fearful of lateness, surmising a middle-aged woman gesticulating for her children needing their milk for breakfast. Maybe my mind's way of interpreting previous painful traumatic experiences; igniting this irrational thought process. Often the round finished so prematurely I'd have to park up, too early to return. The harder I worked, still out-performing, delivering in more ways than one. They would rank up the responsibility and size of round. Weeks into this new job with the largest round of fifty rounds bestowed upon. Fifty crates of milk, two thousand bottles: tower blocks, flats, and miles of walking. Still nailed it. Wondering if all the energy and intent of succeeding had been well thought out; appearing counter-intuitive. The manager, a difficult man. Micro manager. Needing to know all minutiae of what you've done and not done. Instilled so much fear into the employees that a necessity to report back to him some event which had or not occurred. The milk floats were particularly awkward to drive, electronic and battery-powered. They'd jerk from a standing stop, sometimes more forward than anticipated or intended. Then on the second impression of the accelerator, another click on the pedal exceeding the first with a little more gusto. Getting it out of the garage in the morning a cumbersome task. Dozens of other floats side by side, battery-chargers, and storage equipment. So desperate, and worried about punctuality out of the depot and getting into trouble. Panic and irrational desperation would rule. Bang. Hit something. Okay, I'll back up. Bang. Hit something now at the rear. "Shit!" The self-punishment kicked in, berating, criticising. Idiot. Can't you do anything right? Continuing the day's work, bruised and battered confidence. Knowing at the back of my mind, he'd hear about it. Summoned to the office. Another almighty accident while on the round. A car in front and a car behind while delivering to the doorstep. The only way out; reverse up a few yards. Then depart the front. This particular float from a bygone age. Possibly the sixties. Inconceivable, but the pedals placed in reverse position to standard vehicle operation standards. The brake pedal on the right hand side and the accelerator on the left. Similar, to the two-legged chair débâcle at school, my mind would interpret in a binary logical format. Looking backwards my mind would alternate the pedals. If right is for brake looking forward, then right must be accelerator backwards. For example, two negatives equal a positive. The inverse of the input. Proceeding to follow my thought and subtly depressed the reverse pedal. The float moved back slowly as intended. Nearing the car at the rear, my instincts reacted accordingly.

Jumping hard on the brake so as not to hit the car. Low and behold the bloody thing shot back at a rocket pace with a huge smash, thud, wallop, and bang. Glass shattering all over the floor. In my mind's sight: two reverses equal a forward. The unenviable task awaited. Finding the owner of the vehicle, knock on the door and inform them,

"Sorry Mr, but I've just smashed your car up!"

The seeds sown from a bygone era beginning to take root and germinate. Inadequacy, loneliness, poor self-image, and alienation. Days were long performing the milk-run, working in isolation for up to twelve hours, including the journey home. The circumstances and legacy tribulations would portend an orphan without a single relationship or guardian. Missing a wife at home or loving family to greet, and learn how the day had transpired. An absence of life itself. A struggle: but it always had been. This is what I do. In the midst of opposition, obstacle, hindrance, soldier on. During this period of persistently outperforming six days per week, every week void of complaint, a letter had arrived from the hundreds written in the preceding months. An invite to interview for a Despatch Operative at Warburtons bakery. Required to work five or six nights per week, double the money of the milk job, and only a ten-minute drive from home. Plus, indoors opposed out in all weathers in some crappy old float. Breaking down with a depleted battery after having the wipers and lights on all day due to the torrential rain. Worth a shot. A formal interview still pending, so indefinite yet by any means, but definitely worth going for. Extricating self from this oppressive manager, ungodly early mornings could earn more, save more, and get a better car. It had gone in my favour, working for a bakery previously. The letter had arrived speculatively, so unadvertised as such. Only two of us in the running. A pretty straight forward affair. How difficult could an interview be for packing bread and loading onto vans in a despatch environment? To my amazement offered the role, and started a week later after giving notice to the dairy. A pretty laid back affair. Working at night, with absent managers or office staff. Just the bakers, engineers, and the despatch lads. We would operate the pedestrian fork-lift trucks. The ones you stand on the back with the manoeuvre and controls in front. An abundance of thinking time. Reviewing position and status in life, making assessments of progress or lack thereof. Contemplating family, social aspects, identity, and purpose. The journey from inside the bakery to the vans outside, my mind would fantasise. I'm better than this. This isn't me, only a stop-gap. Humming a tune in my head from the 'Working Girl', Hollywood movie with Melanie Griffith. "HHHmmmmm tralalala." Paraphrased as inspiration, aspiration, optimism, positivity, hope, progression, growth, and advancement. A somebody versus nobody. Succeed even if have to claw, fight, sweat blood and tears my way through. Yes I can. Such a private person, these thoughts exclusive to God himself.

Exempt of social outlet during this period at Warburtons. Lucky to go out on a Saturday night. Since my age had eclipsed the proverbial eighteen-years-old threshold. Now okay to frequent the local pub legally. Seemingly, the thing to do, as the majority of my age group, particularly Josh and Paul would spend most of their weekends there. Peer pressure and a colloquial cultural expectation to conform. But once there, the enemy within would appear, powers and principalities of fear, abuse, neglect, rejection, social anxiety, and paranoia would come to life. Inanimate, perplexed, and mute. As though a kettle of vultures circle above and all around. Scrutinising my every move, piercing eyes, judging, condemning, criticising. The more I stood indifferent, odd-looking, unusually quiet for a pub, more paranoid, and conscious. Continuing and perpetuating every moment. Paralysed by mouth and limbs also, facial expressions, and body language. Immutable. A surreal spiritual experience. Given that unidentified or seen by teachers, family or casual acquaintances; the polar opposite. Now it appears everyone in the room is staring directly, even the walls and ceiling are glaring, optics and the bar staff too. The world has turned in on me.

Scant invites, inclusion to any social gatherings or events that occurring locally. Bonfire night: uninvited. A friend of a friend's party: avoided. A lock-in opportunity after hours at the local pub: asked to leave. The day trips to theme parks, markets, or places of interest: left behind. Excluded. The pondering at work would lead to disillusionment: a sense of lost, purposeless, desolate, sad, angry and generally unhappy. Almost resentful. But of what, why, and where was unknown.

The weeks and months mundane, predictable, and uneventful. A dearth of responsibility, stimulus, or challenge. Notwithstanding an opportunity of promotion. The Union had failed to approach me on commencement of service. Seemingly, an administrative oversight membership had been overlooked. A non-member. It wouldn't have been an issue under normal circumstances. The Union had called a strike; out of the blue. Ill-informed, working nights. Missing the snippets of information during office hours. By the time I was made aware: too late. Two days away. A one-day strike. The foreman, Frank, had warned it was a sackable offence, working during the strike, as a non-member. This resonated in a real way. Not in dis-agreement with the pay dispute which was the core issue for opting to strike. But my job is at stake. If my absence is known and also the lack of membership then could be for the chop. I'll have to work to save my job. Unpopular but what can I do? It would necessitate crossing the picket line. Something hadn't encountered prior. It wasn't given a second thought. Maybe my naivety or merely strong moral principles, and a sense of justice. Missing moral or emotional support from home.

"It's up to you!"
"Do what you think is best!"

Gutted. On my own again, taking the world on my shoulders. I had resolved it in my head: all or nothing. I'm not a coward and won't succumb to pressure to go against my well-served intuition. Surprising how many had turned out on the picket line for a dark, cold, damp October night. All men. About thirty of them. Stopped the car in the standard picket-line fashion. The electric window easing its way down.

"I'm going to ask you to turn around!" requested the main union leader.
"This is an official picket line and strongly suggest you turn back!" he went on to say.
"Okay!"
"No problem, but sorry I've got my job to keep!" I asserted.
Drove straight on, parked up and started work as normal.

Only on the other side of the gate within the bakery other colleagues that were Union members had entered through alternative entry points. The rear entrance, back door circumventing the main entrance. I was the only person to cross the line.

An unquantifiable amount of intuition, observation, or analysis could be contrived would prepare for what lay ahead. Unintended consequences, reaping what one has sown or re-actions to actions. Only a one-day strike; the following day back at work. Far from normal. On arrival an atmosphere of indifference. Bowed heads, turned backs, and silent voices. A paradigm shift in attitude and sentiment. Unfriendly, abrasive, and obstructive. Within twenty four-hours the environment unidentifiable. Threats, to smash up my car. Ensuring working life as difficult as possible. Placing obstacles in the way, purposely avoiding. Ignorant to the cultural, social importance of crossing a picket line. The expression of 'black-legged' only known via the news and the great miners' strike. Would I have acted differently knowing I'd be ostracised, rejected, denied, and abandoned by once trusted friends? Probably not. My moral code and self-imposed principles have been bequeathed and honed from a higher being and have served me well to date. Reliable and dependable.

Jack had a very strong constitution, despite the flaws, burdens, brokenness, neglect and alienation. Resolute to the core. Steadfast. A martyr for social justice. Didn't allow the contemporary employees' opposition or enemies to dissuade him from continuing working or to depart. Continuing to turn up diligently, religiously every day, every week, facing the rebellion, objectors, and antagonists. Holding his head high knowing that truth and righteousness would fight his enemies.

Frank was okay with it. He knew the reasons and had almost suggested for me to do it. A sole, lone ally. He had been in the Army for twenty-five years. Was now in retirement but being fifty, still had plenty of energy in him. I'd often sit in the office during a break, eating my 'Snap'. The rest of the workers in the canteen playing cards. We'd naturally connect and enjoy a mutual understanding. A kind of silent surrogate father figure. Good friend. Guiding, advising, and encouraging, which were inexperienced prior. A reverent attitude bestowed upon him. Invited to go walking on a weekend in the Peak District. Induction into the concepts and principles of map-reading, elucidate plants, shrubs, trees, and the natural environment. Informing about the edible and inedible. Use cases for antidotes and survival skills? A whole new world—but loved it. A breath of fresh air. Displaying photographs of his life experience in the Army. Skiing, travelling, rock climbing, different continents visited. Topics learned and the people met along the way. Awe-inspiring. A wholly complete contrast to the current predicament. Rejected at work, rejected at home. A dearth of friends and family, uneducated, anti social, lost, and indifferent. The temptation, allure, and almost envy at his life would appeal. Always had been the adventurer in me: 'Outdoorsy'. Inquisitive, intrepid explorer, curiosity to discover, overcome challenges and live life. Ticking so many boxes: an unprecedented opportunity.

Opportunity, what was that? A chance to be educated, trained in first-aid, mountaineering, orienteering, physical fitness, technology, leadership, survival skills, improve my maths and English. The world would be my oyster. Maybe then I could become a somebody. Possibly rank of corporal or sergeant. But more than that a substitute family. Belonging, identity, purpose, and meaning. The idea mooted to Frank, doubtful he would dismiss it after advocating the forces' lifestyle since acquainted. Emanating from an extraordinarily large family himself and knowing social deprivation. Enthused and willing me to sign up. Thinking, the making of me. A transient thought about the Royal Signals. The life of an infantry man un-alluring. A regiment, challenged mentally, technical expertise a prerequisite, and would stand me in good stead for a future career.

Fully aware of the public perception or reputation of the Army. The infamous basic training, world-renowned for punishing, persecuting, and painful experience. Socially, mentally, emotionally, and physically. The level of fitness and expectation to run miles with heavy boots, fully loaded pack on your back, and carrying a rifle were known. Notwithstanding verbal abuse, insults, berating, 'beasting' and aggression from the cadre of trainers. My eyes were wide open. The intuition was good. You know you're a gentle, softly spoken pacifist, non-aggressive, non-violent person. But cognisant of your inner strengths, character, ability to endure through extreme suffering, persevering in the midst of despair. The fitness you can work on. Preparation and hard work can be invested prior to entry. Doable. If they shout and scream dismiss it and think that's what they do. But already well versed to know what that's like anyway. An exciting thought, the prospect of escaping my contemporary environment to a new life, and beginning. The thought of leaving home was no 'biggy'. Homeless. Game on. A high-risk venture. What if I didn't make it? A forsaken redundant job awaiting on return. It wouldn't be a privilege granted. Once my written notice 'Termination of service', received that was it. No about-turn. Absent of believers. If I don't believe I can, who will?

I presented at the Army Recruitment Office, based in Sheffield. An unprecedented occasion by any stretch of the imagination. Trepidation, reticence, and apprehension stood with me side-by-side. A fusion of mixed feelings, excited but nervous, hopeful but punctuated by temperate doubt. Confident but conscious of the environment entering. Would they be abusive immediately or get me to basic training first? Would the office be toxic with a regimental culture and etiquette? Surely uncivilised? The polar opposite to civilian life. My attire clean and groomed, best it could for a nineteen-year-old boy. Hoping to make a good impression from the off. Unnecessary to shave still boyish. But highly polished shoes, upright posture, and speaking loudly and clearly as my legacy would forbid. A good potential recruit, ticking all the boxes of eligibility. Broken home, poorly educated, single, impressionable, young, malleable, unfocused or direction, and dead-end job. Hailing from Yorkshire. Lacking in skills or vocation. Perfect. The application process involved filling in forms, a tentative interview, general test and full medical. An invitation at a later date for formal interview with a senior rank. That simple. Vacant support and encouragement at home; the norm. A given, Josh and Paul would un-approve or even engage with my achievements or successes. Allowed to get on with the task at hand and gloss over. Similarly, buying my first car all giddy and excited, couldn't wait to tell everyone, overwhelmed with joy. Bright red, immaculately presented Ford Escort. But neglected. Unimpressed. Looking anywhere but at me. Winning a fishing match and had a fifty quid wad in my hand. Five pound the limit up to this moment. Waiving it about as though a gold medal.

"Look at this!" prompted.
"Wonga, wonga!!"
Vacant: brushed off, glossed over, uninterested.

Mum and Dad would note, "Well, it' s up to you!"

Often up to me. Choosing options at school, deny self in favour of 'doing the right thing'. Punishing and persecuting to avoid criticism, insult and injury. Unable to speak. Withdrawn and introverted to avoid conflict, abuse and humiliation from others. To smoke or not. Girlfriend, stay single. Get drunk, stay sober. Aiming to be a perfectionist; appease and pacify family, acquaintances and the general public. Denied of treats or drinks while out. My conditioning taught. Waiting until I got home before consuming refreshment. All up to me.

On my return to work, Frank the first to know; through my zeal. Ecstatic and delighted. In full support and approval of my actions. A good feeling progressing and advancing in life. The incredulous phenomenon of one believing in you. An anxious waiting period, inevitably. Both in terms of disappointment if unsuccessful but also if on the contrary, successful, the life changing-experience that would ensue. Several weeks elapsed while details were vetted and interview notes scrutinised. A letter arrived through the letter box. This was it:

"We can confirm that you have been accepted into the Regiment Royal Signals".

But still yet another appointment. Swear on the oath and grant my allegiance to the Queen. Within the letter were the date and location of reception for the first day of service. 6 May 1992, Catterick Garrison. That was it, two months to prepare myself mentally, physically, and psychologically. Owning an innate critical regime, self-discipline, and motivation to push oneself to the standards acceptable either a blessing in disguise or unwelcome adversary. In spite of the aforementioned passive, gentle, sensitive, softly spoken individual. Synonyms with an archetypal soldier. Uncompromising level of self-control. The extraordinary ability to deny oneself and sacrifice. Unrelenting pressure of must work harder, run faster and longer, keep going, cease to capitulate, achieve, succeed, and strive. The ability to self motivate; absent instruction or prompting. A desire to do right, conform and submit. Although a disparity. Back to binary logic. A plus and a minus. A positive equation at least.

Required to submit notice at Warburtons. A one-to-one meeting arranged with the Despatch Manager. Discuss reasons for departure and possibility of failure; an opportunity to return. The reply, a resounding, "No!" John knew Frank, the life lived and who he'd become. Also known other men who had tried their hand at military life and failed. Recounting their experiences. In a jovial humorous tone. Making light of their flaws, ineptitude, and incompetence.

"This particular guy partaking in drill. His beret sliding down his face, the ornate embroidery that goes over the shoulder and under-arm, loose and falling away. Out of step, creased trousers, and unable to dress appropriately."

Unsure if an endorsement of encouragement or surreptitious ridicule. Almost prophetic. Resonating as though a supernatural premonition. This is me he's talking about in the future, isn't it? my mind questioned. The story has been foretold. Convicted then and there as though lived this experience in the future and now the present, in the past.

Within days of the news hitting, a catalyst to commence my own regimented personal training programme. Jogging. During leisure time driving out to a local reservoir, approximately three miles in circumference. The agenda set. Counting the weeks down, gauging performance, knowing the average pace expected, seven-minute miles. That was the goal. Running in all weathers, cold, frost, snow, rain, sun, and heat. Often opt for the more challenging route up-hill; arduous as possible. Religiously, sometimes four times per week, every weekend, every week. Press-ups, sit-ups in my room, and lifting weights. Thinking, if they could be pacified or appeased by my excellent turn-out, exemplary athletic fitness prior to induction of training, already in excellent condition. Then maybe, just maybe, some of the verbal abuse and insults could wane or at least mitigate. Presenting on the day as the consummate soldier.

Mum and Dad would drive me to the train station for the ultimate departure. A rare occasion by any means, a lift and supported, unprecedented. A momentous occasion. Twenty years old, leaving home, every artefact known left behind. Possessions although few. The car would have to go. Tackle could stay in the loft but I'd miss it nonetheless. Home as I knew it. The rituals and routines, local culture, and acquaintances. But also leaving home to join the Army. Would I ever return? Where will they send me? What if war breaks out? Mum in tears as the train pulled in to the platform. Dad passive and inanimate as ever. Indifferent. My demeanour nonchalance. Don't see what the big deal is. This is my ticket out of this hole and to a new life. Giddy, if wasn't about to get on a train to initiate in ten weeks of hellish demeaning, brainwashing, torture. Relinquishing civilian life, freedom, rights, choice, security, and protection.

A solemn journey en route to the barracks. Time to think and ponder. Life. Would I be missed? Psyching myself up for the 'What ifs'. What would the other guys be like? How violent and abusive will some of the corporals be? What would the reception be like on discharge or Personal Voluntary Release (PVR). Greeted at the local train station by corporals in civilian dress, inconspicuously diverting unwanted attention. Once identified, registered, and credentials checked; off to a stark reality check from civilian life. Crossing the entrance comparable to a border-crossing point. Once signed up capitulate norms, beliefs, values and knowledge you had acquired in life. The cultural civilian nuances, liberty, and rights. Laws and rules change. Once your right, no longer. To roam and be free; leave and return. Rise and fall as you wish. Now under military law. Once through the entrance, at the mercy of all who had authority. A raw-recruit, 'squaddie', would approximate everyone.

Immediately on arrival the atmosphere notable. Hostile, loud, and aggressive. Shouted at within minutes of dropping the luggage. Assigned rooms and soon to discover which other recruits sharing. Six beds to a room. The following days consumed; measured up for helmets, shoe size, trousers, jackets, height, chest size, and waist. Then the beret would come, followed by instruction, how to make a bed and iron your own clothes, the Army way. Christian names dropped. Known by your number or surname. The change in events in the last twenty-four hours were immense. Catapulted into a foreign zone, socially and environmentally unfamiliar. A paradigm shift in regime change. Sleeping patterns, meal times, activities, work timetable, cleaning, polishing and ironing. Introduced to new terminology, methods, practices, and military jargon. The suggestion of weapons, firing, armoury, the guard room and, beasting. The majority of the recruits had previous experience; the cadets or Territorial Army. Familiar with drill, webbing, berets, expectations, standards, and military culture. In stark contrast to my abyss of knowledge. Ignorant and unknowing of Army culture. In at the deep end. Drill, an unknown phenomenon; practised or taught prior. The respect one should bestow a senior rank; alien. Dos and don'ts unfamiliar, kit foreign and rifle unseen before.

My people-pleasing and approval-seeking tendencies would kick in, big-time. In spite of poor understanding and ultimate ignorance of what I had let myself in for. Vying to be liked, approved of, validated, and valued. Arrived at the wrong place. Never going to happen. You're not going to be liked or approved of. This is the Army. But still eager to please, do the right thing. Be good. Manifesting, aiming for a perfectionist attitude. Striving, far beyond the mean or considered normal. Rocketing through moving averages into a stratospheric zone of unattainable matter. Must do better, try harder, improve, refine, and excel. The unfortunate counter to this methodology; quite the opposite. Overshoot, excel but to the point rendered failing. The impetus to try harder, do better, aim for acceptance and approval. The cycle would repeat.

While practising drill my whole upper body would stiffen. A concoction of stress, anxiety, fear of failure, and abuse. The pressure and responsibility to get it right. Surrounded by sixty other recruits and a sergeant with his pace stick. The adrenaline would almost paralyse in stiffness.

"By the left, quick march!" went the command.

Marching is like walking. It's the most natural phenomenon known to man. You don't have to do anything, merely walk and arms will naturally swing in an ordered motion. When upper body, including arms, is rigid it is impossible to march. An unnatural swinging occurs. Forced, controlled and inhibited. By that virtue, it renders the process untenable. Failing. Intermittently both arms would swing in tandem, out of sync, or uncoordinated with the rest, the appearance of a child's robotic action-man.

"Jones!! F*** off!
Get out of my f***ing sight, you waste of f***ing space!"

Then, if that wasn't enough. Making it more complicated by turning corners.

Two weeks in and the intolerable regime taking its toll. Eighteen hour days, up at five, cleaning, washing, polishing, ironing, running, circuit training, drill, weaponry, lectures and so on. Exhausted physically, mentally and emotionally. The social antithesis. In a family of sorts, but mistrusting or failing to bond. An inability to connect. Alienation in the midst of dozens of others. Monday morning partaking in drill, due to the non-fortuity of randomness my position within the rank at the front, particularly out of my comfort zone. Safe and secure at the back. There, my cock-ups, mistakes, and errors could be hidden or bypassed. But on this occasion I was lead.

"By the left, quick march!" commanded the Sergeant.

My limbs were able to conform sufficiently so that attention was unwarranted. Everything going dandy, almost feeling good about it. But the exhaustion caught up, despite outdoors in the fresh air, marching with sixty other recruits. I was nodding off.

A faint, albeit subdued "Right wheel!" heard in my head.
Again. "Right wheel!"
Still continuing in an onward direction.
"Righhhttt f***ing wheel!"

Missed it hook, line, and sinker. The Corporal almost flattened me. Jumped on top and pummelled me to the ground.

"What the f*** are you doing, you f***ing ignoramus?"

From this outburst the whole troop became arch-rivals. I had let the side down. Underperforming. The weak link. Taunting, critical, insulting, and generally belligerent. My reputation would precede me: weak, failing, flawed, clumsy, and lacking co-ordination. An inept and incompetent soldier. That's how my mind would perceive and receive.

While in the barracks, we'd have to prepare our kit. Sew if necessary. If your back pocket happened to be unbuttoned they'd rip it off to make an example. That's where the sewing came in. But embroidery and military paraphernalia adorned to our garments required stitching. Another random, obscure, unpalatable doctrine.

I would present to the Sergeant as:

"Excuse me, Sergeant would it be possible to borrow the scissors please?"
"F*** off, Jones!"

Ceremonial inspections a truism, standard routine, first thing in the morning, daily. 7:00 a.m sharp. On waking required to wash and shave, clean the ablutions to an immaculate standard as these too inspected. Attend the NAAFI for breakfast. Return to your room and prepare for the impending onslaught of abuse. The majority of the work accomplished the night before, cleaning and polishing the floor, removing every remnant of dust, ironing, presenting our kit in its most pristine condition. Mopping and polishing the main corridor until you could see your face in it. My ignorance also extended to the unattainable standards expected. Deemed 'neat and tidy' was a 'shit state' to the instructors. My judgements were wide of the mark and wholly unacceptable to the regiment's lofty creed. The first week was probably the worst. Missing an inkling of what lay ahead. Unavailable and unattainable recommended guides, tutorials, top ten tips, or an advisory on how one should present his locker upon inspection within the Army. The clothes and garments were pressed, kit and helmet in place. The boots had had eight hours spent on them, they must pass for that fact alone. It was a no-brainer. What could they possibly have issue with?

My countenance on inspection was one of fear and trepidation. Apprehensive. Hearing the calamitous row and wanton aggression that resonated from several rooms down the corridor. Expletives and profanities, insults, sounds of breaking objects, smashing and crashing, slamming of doors, and missiles being launched. This was on approach and almost imminent arrival at our room.

"Room room shun!"

We all stood to attention as had been instructed. At least primed by the forthcoming tornado, indiscriminate violent destruction of contemporary artefacts. On entry to the room the atmosphere altered. Clenched fists, tight chest, braced, and expectant. As the Corporal would meander around the room appearing to find fault, discover an oversight, error, speck of dust and doing his duty.

My heart rate would regulate to the potential threat in terms of warm or cold. Similarly to the childhood games when seeking an object out. The closer he came to the locker or to me personally it would increase in regularity. The fight or flight phenomenon. He had already criticised one of the other recruits for some innocuous unforeseen absence of equipment. They'd find dust although a vacuum. On arrival at my locker, within seconds every single item trashed, screwed up, thrown across the room, flying boots, in all directions, cursing, swearing, and insulting along the way.

Two weeks in when it happened. The great revelation. Appreciative of how the Army works, now in a position of insight to gauge my adaptability, compatibility, and worthiness as a potential competent soldier. Ultimately, the core principle of the Army is based on serving. Peers, seniors, troop, regiment, country, and the Queen. The revelation presented a significant and stark distinction. The legacy and history that had brought me here would have impacted. That self-preservation was paramount and sacrosanct. Foreign and unacquainted to serving others. Who would I serve? From birth primary focus and human need is to survive. To think, provide, and make safe for oneself. The notion of a shared responsibility, teamwork, family dynamics, providing for each other was alien. The intuition excellent again. It had alluded to an insidious discrimination. The personal profile exhibited and the one expected in the Army were poles apart. Moreover, unable to adapt, modify or fix. The giant encumbered greater than me. A very definite and purposeful phenomenon. Locked and bound. Specific moments which confirmed the intelligence. When an artefact had to be collected. My behaviour and conditioning would look after self and get my own. The others would fetch and carry for each other. I could see how it should be done and would like to partake but couldn't bring myself to practically implement it. But here now. Going to have to soldier on and do the right thing.

John's prophetic insight came to pass. Unable to conform, inadequately performing tasks, substandard, out of step, uncoordinated, clumsy and lacking attention to detail. Ignorant of military etiquette, rules, and values. Randomly, the corporal would waltz into the room unannounced; preparing kit for the following morning's inspection. My head lost in a world of polishing the toe cap of my boots which had occupied for the previous two hours. All the other recruits in the room shot up and stood to attention. Seemingly bizarre why they had all done that, only me sat down. Got another 'bollocking'.

"So, you think you're different, do you Jones? Beyond showing due respect to a senior rank?"

By the third week, committing so many errors of judgement, cock-ups, oversights, lapses of concentration, missed steps, and pointing my rifle at the corporal. As well as the proverbial sub-standard boot shine. They put me on 'show-parade', every evening, all week. Show-parade is when you are required to attend the guard room promptly. There, reside military police. The sole purpose is to beast, ensure suffering, never forget this evening not for a few days but your entire life. Ridicule and berate your heritage, name, family, home town, looks, height, hair, voice, anything to break and undermine who you are. The insidious traits of formative years still salient within my soul. To out-perform, seek approval, get it right, achieve, succeed. Win at any cost. The guardsmen ordering me back to barracks to get a toothbrush and return within two minutes. It couldn't be done. Even if I sprinted all the way and back again; up to the wire. But fear of failing, bad, dis-liked, and disapproved, was too great. I'd have to make it. Sweat pouring from my forehead on arrival at the barracks, panting and almost hyperventilating. I'd get the chosen item and sprint all the way back, nearly breaking my neck and causing an accident en route. No time to look at my watch, absent. On my return, impossible to speak, catching my breath, bent over double.

"Get up, you f***ing waste of space!" they would yell.
"You are ten seconds late!"

The routine enduring all night. Back and forth, having to fetch an artefact or item of clothing pressed and presented, to be disparaged and punished yet again. Every evening after a full day's training, running miles, inspection, lecture, rifle practice, drill, circuit training, cleaning, and polishing. A young guy that had passed out with the previous troop. Appointed student-assistant to support the corporals and sergeant in their endeavour to turn us into fighting soldiers. He wasn't for us, but against. Aggressive, abrasive, and brutal. Retaining a regular nick-name for me. F***wit. Whenever our paths crossed or within speaking distance, the term presented as greeting. My twenty-first birthday only a few days away. Difficult not conceal as deemed as special as the eighteenth. But acknowledged and mirror back who I am and what I am. It felt as though I needed to say those few words. I'm twenty one today! For my own sanity. Unable to say those words, unthinkable. Burdened, carrying that thought alone in my head. Informing what I thought to be an ally. Although couldn't trust anyone. My naivety and innocence let me down. Mooted through rumours that recruits capture, bind, strip, humiliate, and degrade the incumbent in some kind of birthday celebration ritual. A regimental bath. Which could conceivably end up in a bath. Forty guys within the troop. Didn't bare thinking about. My defences primed. Inconceivable this event ever going to happen. I'll give it my all to defend despite there potentially being multiple adversaries. If I have to smash them in the head or stab someone, so be it. Much of the day spent cleaning. I'd have to watch my back all day. At any moment I could be accosted, pinned to the ground and they'd have me. The day passed uneventful.

Roll-call everyday to account for missing persons or AWOL. Rank and file of recruits against the wall on the wing. The instructor's gave the order to call out a number from one, dependent on the index.

"One, two, three, four ..." etc..

I had never shouted or raised my voice in my entire life. Always soft, quiet and monotonous. An omission of feeling, passion, or life. An almost empty voice. Weak and feeble. An invisible glass ceiling impossible to breach.

"Fifteen!" spoken in my normal voice as though I was talking to my neighbour.
"Halt!" yelled the Corporal.
"I can't hear you, shout out again!" he remonstrated.

A smidgen louder.
"Fifteen!"
"Shout it out it again!"
A smidgen louder again.
"Fifteen!"
"I still can't hear you!"
"Fift f***ing teen!"

The first time and obviously the loudest a sound had left my lungs and mouth since birth. Euphoric and liberated. I can shout. Yes I can. Enjoyable too. Shouting was going to have to develop pretty fast if I was going to give orders. Move a troop of men and get them to stop-start and turn.

Mail was delivered to the barracks from 'civvy-street'. Missing a girlfriend only Mum writing. All the other recruits would receive letters from their respective girlfriends. The

Corporal tasked with distribution noted the style and presentation of handwriting.

“This is his mother’s, I can tell!” he pronounced to the waiting troop.

My Nan had also written despite modest connection. These letters merely confirmed my intuition had allayed all these years. How distant and unknowing they were. A lack of engagement. Totally alien to my feelings, fears, and insecurities. For all intents and purposes, written from complete strangers. As they used to do in World War I. The authorities would encourage single women on the mainland to write to soldiers in the trenches to imbue moral support. But these were random, alien, and aloof. Revealing cosmetic trivia back home. Desperate to be heard. How horrific my experience is, jumping off twelve foot walls in an instant. Running for miles while in pain, throwing up and difficulty breathing. Fellow comrades dismissed for losing their mind. Sat in jail for hours as my boots substandard. Bullied by other recruits but also the instructors. Unacquainted with anyone to defend or fight my corner.

The following week the Corporal and Sergeant would carry out the morning inspection. Over previous weeks, a reputation had attached itself. My name appearing on multiple occasions. Jones this, Jones that, would pop up everywhere a problem.

“I’ve had enough of Jones!” said the Sergeant.

One of their most inhumane acts to grant the privilege of wearing a contrarian, prized, coveted headwear; akin to a mountaineer’s helmet, in white. Although adorned with fluorescent orange paint with the words, ‘Four Troop Fezzer!’, daubed on the front for all to see. The terms and conditions were to wear it all day from dawn till dusk. To the toilet, the NAAFI, drill, barracks, rifle-range, show-parade, and anywhere that day may take you. The purpose: to degrade, humiliate, and break a person's spirit. This helmet allocated to me. I knew a line had eclipsed whereby evidently unbearable. My final line. It would finish me off. Bordering on mental abuse and torture, public humiliation at best. By the Grace of God, another recruit found more deserving and bequeathed to him. An escape never to be forgotten. But nonetheless, knowing my days were numbered. The relentless abuse, long hours, bullying, isolation, knowing my indifference, unable to contribute to family dynamics. A union. The pressure beginning to manifest. Shaking and trembling on inspection. Aware how the legacy had undermined my ability to function at this level and rendered broken. But only by inherent self awareness and insight. The questionnaire on application should have alerted me. Mental health—yes or no?

In spite of my human failings there were tasks accomplished to expectation. The physical element: always did well running, circuit training, marching for long distances, carrying our kit. During a running session; asked to stop for a while. The purpose to have a race. A mere one hundred yards. But had to compete and return to the start as fast as possible. Invariably, give my all. That was the key to my downfall. Striving and vying for perfection. The instructors weren't daft. They could spot a worker or a shirker. Their years of experience doing the job could discriminate a recruit going the extra mile or coasting along. The Corporal asked the recruits as I passed the finish line:

"Who's he? What's his name?"

Shit, I thought, in for it again. What did I do this time?

Unmentioned. Strange, why would he want to know who I am? Surely, if I'd screwed up they'd let me know about it.

The appropriate chain of command made aware of my distress. As much as they flogged and cursed, unwilling for me to leave. Convincing to stay despite the regular punishing and critical routines. An arduous, cumbersome, and protracted procedure, dis-charging (PVR) of oneself. Necessitate a whole process of meetings or appointments with differing levels of seniority or rank. Beginning at the bottom, Corporal. Mum and Dad would drive up to the barracks one weekend for some moral support. But again, overwhelmingly disappointed.

"Well, it's up to you. It's your choice!"
"We can't tell you what to do!"
"What do you think?"

The decision on my shoulders, as everything in life had been. Overwhelming evidence in my psyche it wasn't to be. The revelation, obvious brokenness, my inner-being exposed to me, caring, compassionate, tolerant, forgiving, sensitive, passive, and pacifist. The problems that ran deeply within. The realisation, a social misfit, mistrust, fail to depend, or rely on anyone. Issues with fear, hyper-vigilant, weak and vulnerable. Didn't equate to the stereotypical soldier. In an ideal world would have progressed and overcome the difficulties. But this is profoundly more reverent than any vocation, employment or internship. Was there more to the motive of joining up than a curiosity to see the world, an education, and family? Well, I've made the decision. I'm out! Let's do it. The inevitable fallout on re-instatement back at Warburtons. Albeit employed on a casual ad hoc, as and when required basis.

"Failed, couldn't handle it!" they'll say.

I'll deal with it. I'm a better man acknowledging my defeat, admitting failure, and facing the music too.

INTO THE WILD

Mum and Dad would take me out to dinner on arrival home. A conciliatory action on their part. But served to add to my disillusionment of family. Sat in silence. Counter-intuitive. Paradoxical. Served but resenting the occasion and atmosphere. The duty of it. An absence of heart. Distant, aloof, and dis-engaged. Never mirrored back the horror, enduring torture, torment, verbal and mental abuse. The physical endurance my body had been exposed to, relentless "beasting", drill, and show-parade. Unaware, the incapacity and incomprehension to absorb and digest the essence of it. Like it had never happened.

"You don't look very happy to say you've just come out!" Mum said curiously.

Having left the conflict, another conflict had revealed itself. The jubilation of freedom and liberation but the disappointing fact—back to reality. A dysfunctional home, brothers unspoken, mundane job with little stimulus and hope of prospects, education, or prosperous future. Nonetheless, a passion for more. Something in my belly would hunger and yearn to reach what seemed an unattainable destination. To find the true self. To cast off every trait that had become the other me. Leave behind the 'old self'. The baggage, oppression, anxiety, paranoia, low self-esteem, loathing, anti-social and a tormented soul. Aware more in me than packing or delivering bread. A mind that needed stimulating.

Jack was so damaged his mind and soul had shut-down. Unbeknown to him. Instituting a moral, legalistic, rigid binary code. Manifested in his thinking, behaviour, attitude, actions: whether to relate or not. Accept or reject. A great hindrance. An inability to give or receive, praise, or compliment.

Appreciate, value, intimate or make friends. Reinforced by underlying spiritual powers: hate, envy, pain, suffering, loss, grief, sorrow, unloved, neglect, and alienation. The thought would call the pain to action and vice versa. A labyrinth of border and boundary walls. Solidifying and securing the congenial essence. Feeling couldn't feel or breathe. Emotion never saw the light of day, incarcerated. Spiritual, stifled and shackled; immutable.

From unspent monies received by HM Forces and proceeds from the sale of the car. A few thousand pounds had accumulated in the bank. During school activity period I had shown an interest towards computing. Whether authentic or one born out of solitude, avoidance of people and ultimate escape. Alluring. Only playing games, unlike today's advanced hardware and software technology, this was BBC Basic, in every sense of the word. Hitherto, my introduction to computing. Inserting disks, loading programs and entering input. An advert in the press had caught my eye. Train to be a COBOL programmer. A distance learning or correspondence course. The salary expectations on completion were blazoned all over the ad. Huge for what seemed little effort. Clueless to the academic rigour expected. Vacant prior knowledge or experience at school, all but failing in maths. That fact would render unqualified for attending the computing subject. The application should never have been made. They would fleece me of my hard-earned cash. A dearth of elders, superiors, guardians, or relatives who would offer endorsement, protect my naivety and exhort to do the right thing. Another desperate attempt to survive and save oneself. To yield providence, security, dignity, and well-being. What did I have to lose other than two thousand quid? I'm in. Shit or bust.

The four huge ring binders would arrive in the post. A very daunting prospect, given the metaphorical visualisation. Bulky, intimidating, packed full of paper, depicting knowledge, professionalism, business, or reverent paradigm. What one might see on the news as the ambassadors and dignitaries gather for a UN meeting. Just the sight of it seemed superior and advanced without even opening the contents. A surreal moment. A clash of realism hit. Self-doubt, under dog, poor academic track record, void of self-belief. Presented with an opportunity to counter those beliefs, maybe a break to become a somebody. Laying down what had gone before. To sow a seed of reaching my full potential, to become the man always destined to be. To get from current position to intended destination, there is going to be contention, fights, battles, opposition, and surreal moments. This is the beginning. No turning back. The journey too great to be fickle and feeble. You are going to have to dig deep into those recesses of your soul, that go to extremes.

Warburtons did take me back, albeit on a ‘casual basis’. Temping, working on an ad hoc basis, as and when required. This suited, as it allowed me to study but also gave me enough money to live on for the week. A common occurrence was for me to return home from a night shift at six in the morning and get the teaching aids and learning resources out and study prior to going to bed. Bits, bytes, kilobytes, and megabytes. Computer logic, binary, languages, data records, statements and the fundamentals of computing. Absent of teachers or tutors, self-taught—literally. Reading the most mundane, uninspiring tenets. Office automation, a data field, the construct of data, file organisation, data management storage and retrieval. The days before email, you’d have to submit hand written work manually through the post. A two-to-three-week turn around was the average. My starting point inadequate, ill equipped and ill-informed. Plenty of mistakes to correct; rendered a laborious, protracted process of back and forth until eventually the penny dropped and retained the most basic knowledge.

Absent of friends and acquaintances on my return back to civilian life, my only means of meeting social needs were to tag along with Josh to the local pubs in the village. Missing an official invite or zeal to include me. I’d have to beg. The

Army had done many things to me but hadn't yielded a voice, inner peace, self-esteem or contentment. On the contrary. Welcomed on terms, and I don't get above my station, speak, gain attention, or take the spotlight off him. Unspoken rules of course. A look enough. But then the aura: spiritual atmosphere. The body language. Stoic, abrupt, and displeased. A frown and a scowl. Wasn't so much what was said but wasn't. The silence. My place well known, gained from the bygone years. Submissive, unspoken, unseen. Synonymous to the electric fence used to control cattle. Veer near to the no-go zone and you get zapped. Well acquainted with my zones, boundaries, and no-go territories. This compounded the bondage. Mute from the beginning but daring to speak would see me shot down in flames. Ironic. A welcomed companion in the midst of being despised, resented, and loathed. Suffering and enduring me to appear, out with 'mates', as opposed to the proverbial 'saddo', sat drinking at the bar alone. The first night, my senses on high alert. A new situation, unfamiliar people. Curious how Josh's behaviour will play out. The best tactic to stay shtum, then at least can't look or sound stupid. But invariably, unspoken regardless. It wouldn't give cause to berate, mock, or insult. Then it came. Hadn't said a word. One of the bar-maids talking about me.

One said, "He's not at the back of the door!"
Another noted, "He looks like he's come from the back of the garden shed to me!"

Served at the bar was a stressful encounter. The trepidation of communication, making a request confidently and clearly. Mumble and fumble, stuttering along the way. Joking under their breathe between each other. Becoming a familiar experience to be mocked and ridiculed for being mute. The proverbial joke when vacant in conversation. The number of sarcastic comments.
"Will you keep quiet?"
"He never shuts up, does he?"

Beginning to hate self. The way I was. How frustrated, untenable the situation is. Impossible to communicate what it is. But with whom would I converse anyway? Hating the way I am and have become.

Despite the hell that had consumed me, a shaft of light would emerge in the guise of one of the associate's girlfriend. Angelic, not in appearance, but a friendly silent companion. Silent in the sense that the immediate social environment was without witness. A connection: mutually endearing nature and understanding of each other would ensue. Something special took place in these precious moments. A catalyst to be seen, heard, and understood about the most trifling, mundane, minutiae, aspects of life. Ate at lunch, taste, likes vs dislikes, whether the crust was left over. Making light of one's foibles and quirks. Sharing similar views on music, radio shows, times, having an epiphany of liking one and others' company and personas. We would share these intimate, private exchanges in the midst of everyone else in the busy pub. Her boyfriend at her side. Able to whisper at close proximity and either by the loud music or equally noisy pub chatter we were inaudible. Concealing our private up-close and personal discourse, unwittingly. Null scores on my tally chart of scoring. Pulling a bird, by Yorkshire's own vernacular dialect, or dating a member of the opposite sex. My chart was 'blankety blank'. Retrospectively, an allure to a particular girl, my mind would get ahead of itself. The obsessive, irrational, dysfunctional elements within would take hold. Fantasising. All loved up. How I'd do the right thing. Open doors, polite, serve, and wait on her like a proper gentleman. A perfect scenario. She would want for nothing. Meeting her every request. A white knight or prince charming. We'd get married, honeymoon, have kids, and live happily ever after in the perfect family. All loved up.

This familiar routine would repeat itself with Hillary. Thinking about her all week. Hoping to get a glimpse at the weekend. Two minutes would do me. Could live on the ecstasy for the whole week until the next encounter. A smile from the other side of the pub would complement too. My heart would race as she walked through the door. Pretending not to look desperately or appear staring. But it's all that I would think about. Increasingly excited the closer she manoeuvred around the pub. Until the ultimate moment, she would have to pass me. The pinnacle of the night. Over in seconds and the fallout would ensue. Disappointment, sorrow, and sadness. That's it till maybe next week. The legalistic, binary, logical mind would contrive the 'ideal' scenario. Fantasising, essentially about love. This would go on beyond a year. Redundant in my ability to act appropriately. Knowing full well she had a boyfriend: that he also knew me. But the shared experience I had was unprecedented. To be seen for me, innocence, vulnerability, mannerisms, and idiosyncrasies. We once had a snog on New Year's Eve. Uncoordinated, unplanned, and unashamed. Unmentioned afterwards and life carried on.

Desperate for a well-earned break upon departing the Army, decided that a shared acquaintance, Josh, and me would take a week's holiday to Ibiza, Balearic Islands. Unusual in that he couldn't bare to be around me at the best of times. But having many years experience of it, I knew the drill. Unable to bring himself to go with Nigel alone. Too awkward. Couldn't wander off at will and do his own thing. Three, more palatable. More conversation and shared experience compared to two. On that premise allowed to partake. Unsurprisingly, Josh barely looked at me all week. The predictable austere body language. An air of resentment, enduring, and suffering me yet again. Obviously only there as a place-holder. A convenience. Towards the end of the week, word had reached Josh that Hillary was leaving her boyfriend and was in love with me. To hear those words beyond surreal. Unloved and unwanted. A phenomenon in itself. For someone to forsake their boyfriend for me. That was a first. Incredulous. Astounded. Beside myself. Impossible to react. Too good to be true. Void of any good luck, providence, mercy, grace, or anything of the like. I'd have to wait till we get back home and hear it first hand before I could seriously absorb the news.

The first weekend post-arrival back home from Ibiza; the point of illumination. The truth exposed and I'd know one way or the other. Hillary was present, had apparently been a regular visitor in my absence and this the foundation for us to get it on. An omission of obvious reference to the dynamics of ending one relationship and entering another. We were relaxed and casual. Still trying to come to terms with the news. Although my mind and heart had raced ahead and gone head over heels in excitement. Her taxi beeped outside to take her home. She sat nonchalantly. I sat passively ignorant. Eventually time had elapsed and she had to go.

"See you later!" I said innocently.

The next day I was lambasted by Josh:
"You were supposed to walk her to the car and snog her at the back while you were out there, you f****ing idiot!"

"What?" replied bemused.

The penny dropped. It wasn't me. Not that shallow or secular. More of a patient gentleman. That will wait for the precious moment and ambience. Another example of being ridiculed and berated for being so innocent, vulnerable, and naïve. Honourable traits. Punishing myself in vain. Too late. An opportunity had passed me by. It would have been lovely to kiss her behind the pub in the dark. But it's just one evening. There will be others. The word had travelled fast. A hot topic as far as the gossip trail went. Before I could meet Hillary again her boyfriend's mother had been calling the house. Displeased at the outcome. Suggesting I had taken Hillary away from her son. My defence was that I'd been out of the country and had only just heard of it.

"You need to speak to her!" duly informed.

This harassment went on for days. Hillary's number was unknown even to communicate or discuss what was going on. My threshold had been reached and enough was enough. Called her ex and suggested we meet. I'll go to his house and we'll have it out once and for all. Presenting the case:

"This is her doing. She has orchestrated all this while I've been away. You need to speak to her. But don't make allegations that I am some kind of girlfriend-snatcher," I asserted confidently and believably. That was it. Never heard from Hillary ever again.

Some months prior, it had seemed fit to scrawl across my fingers, the word 'Hate'. As the stereotypical prisoners do with tattoos. Only this time, a pin without ink. Piercing the skin to release blood, 'h' on the fore of the index finger and 'a', 't', and 'e' on the others.

There were a few guys from Baxters that were still known to me. They would venture down town on a Friday night, drinking in the pubs, bars, and then off to a nightclub. I'd stand in silence. Unable to speak. Often one of the acquaintances of the acquaintances would question:
"Are you okay?"

I'd reply "Hhhmmmm!"

Knowing full well, far from okay. But no nineteen-year-old youth is going to get it.

Strange behaviours led me to believe all was unwell. The geographic location of my self-imposed Army training in Sheffield, Langsett Reservoir, a religious sanctuary albeit unplanned. An oasis tantamount to a second home. It happened over a period. Continuing with jogging despite having left the Army. It was tranquil, peaceful, few people around, and only the cows and sheep for company. I would take refuge, solace, and solitude there too often. At the first sign of tumult, torment, or unrest that was my cue. I'd be there. Running from self. Attempting in vain to crack the code. The encrypted code, indecipherable. Where to begin to resolve, interpret, understand, and ultimately gain insight that would produce the desired output as FREEDOM. Free from the snares, the lies, untruths, the shackles, bondage, mummification, and hysteria. Physically and metaphorically. Unable to live in one's skin. The unbearable spiritual atmosphere in the house. I'd have to escape. The driving around the streets and the self-justification that, I'll go for a drive, became all too frequent. To the point, the majority of my spare time was sat in the car at Langsett Reservoir pondering life and self, perplexed, paranoid and pontificating. Lost, bewildered, and alienated. The weekends, parents would go away to the caravan. Josh and Paul would go away for the weekend with their shared friends. Excluded from all gatherings. I'd be left alone. The loneliness became too much. I knew that the periods without speaking were joining up with other periods of not speaking to the point when weeks were passing by, then months. On occasion, in the pub squeezing the pint glass in my hand, hoping it would break there and then. It never did. Driving was revealing in terms of my psychological and emotional state. On occasion, just put my foot to the floor on the accelerator, for no particular reason. Even in a thirty zone. Visions of driving into brick walls at one hundred mph. Uncaring. Driving on the motorway and imagining randomly swerving into the central reservation from the inside lane. The familiarity and conditioning seemed to portray my lifestyle as normal. It was what I'd known and grown up with. But what lay beneath, had been suppressed, hidden, forgotten, and denied. It was causing ructions within my soul. Approaching a crescendo of full-blown despair.

The following year uneventful. Maybe the calm before the storm. Continuing in the current vein of two or three nights' work at Warburtons, working through laborious studies making moderate progress despite the arduous task of teaching oneself computing by reading reams of paper on the nuances of data models and architecture, semantics, and program logic. Notwithstanding the almost religious compulsion to re-visit the sanctuary. The jogging another significant indicator that all was unwell. It too, becoming an obsessive compulsion. Not a case of jogging for pleasure but to quell my insanity. The pent-up pressure, frustration, and despair could be diffused albeit temporarily. Pacifying and yielding some respite before the next encounter would present itself, usually within two to three days. The compulsive behaviour repeating. The cycle became the norm. Unable to get through the day without exerting energy to self-medicate with adrenaline or endorphins. Complementing the aforementioned, the act of expression, projecting inner rage, anger, hatred, and bitterness would alleviate tension, internal anxiety, and agitation. Synonymous to a volcano. Innocuous tremors. Controlled eruptions that would quickly dissipate. Rumblings and enmity would elucidate their displeasure. The catalyst being envy, jealousy, lack of attention, paranoia, and the metaphorical friends or stowaways that had attached themselves over the years, known as Rage, Despair, and Torment.

An ad in the local press for a computer training course funded by the local Chamber of Commerce. To engage youths not in education or employment. A small step up. Learn to touch-type, databases, spreadsheets, and word processing. Yielding the skills to function in an office environment. Departing the casual role at Warburtons for a more constructive direction to improve oneself. In addition, an industrial placement integrated into the course. Whereby valuable experience could be gained, preparing you for future employment. The appointment assigned to me was for a local import-export company. A disappointing interview if you could call it that. More like an encounter. The manager enquired regarding my whereabouts and origin.

“Born and bred from Sheffield” I said.

"Strong in arm, thick in head, eh?" he replied to great delight, smiling to himself.

We've got one here, I thought.

The first day was approached with trepidation and reticence as standard in this kind of scenario. New people, environment, unfamiliar tasks, processes, telephones, and communicating with other foreign stakeholders. The import-export industry was also a foreign entity to me. The huge desk bestowed to me daunting in its stature. A spiritual aura all of its own. Former residents, previous disgruntled employees who saw fit to leave. A shrine or grave for the predecessors who had graced its surface in bygone years. A desk worn not from knocks and shocks but by the quantity and frequency that had passed over it. It held a transient persona. For all intents and purposes it might as well have had a 'Vacant – Occupied' sign hung upon it. For its flipping from one state to another. As the next naive vulnerable, innocent, placement student would enter office.

Evident from the beginning it wasn't going to work. The intention was for me to practice what I had learned on the course. PC skills, word-processing, databases, and spreadsheets. The manager attempting to teach me the fundamentals of the import-export business within the week. Copious amounts of parcels, envelopes, letters, and any other paraphernalia related to the business. All dumped on my desk. Deemed my responsibility to calculate the currency exchange which had arrived from around the world. Dictating on cargo, shipping lanes, the Far East, containers, and consignments. Surely, you had go to university to study the subject as an industry. I've got it. He wants me here, practically cost free. Exploitation to become one of his subordinates, who will do the majority of the work that would cost £30k per annum to get the right person. His demeanour, attitude, tone, and behaviour also confirmed my initial concerns. Abrupt, cold, and abrasive. An unhappy angry man. He would delegate, informing me to do this and do that. But failing to explain or affirm I have understood. Nonchalantly talking at me. He had told me to send two faxes to two different numbers. Out of worry, self-doubt, and anxiety they were sent to the wrong address. He went mad.

"You've just sent the bloody quote from our supplier to the client!"

He laid into me verbally, insulting, criticising and blaming for the error. That was it. Just walked straight out.

I had had eyes for a girl at the local pub. It often happened that way. The slightest iota of attention and hooked. A euphoria took place. A smile, banter, or sharing trivial conversation. That was all it took. An affinity or allegiance would form, albeit irrational and contrived. Fantasised out of the need to be known, identified, seen, and communicated with. My mind would often get ahead of itself, become irrational, and obverse. Many of my conversations had taken place in my head. Me, myself, and I. The inner voice and conscious became well acquainted. Discussing and debating the trivia of life on a daily basis. Substituting a maternal, paternal, and pastoral role that had been void. Affirming a social justice with my persona. Who was right or wrong. Where fault lay. Them or me. A mechanism to navigate the obstacles of life.

Unprecedented to ask a girl out. The fear of rejection was too great. Lacking in confidence and self-esteem, never going to happen. But the envy and jealousy would present itself, compounded by my own frustrations and social inability to engage. Convincing myself: something there, just a case of time. She had already been back to my parents' house on walking home one night. That must be a signal. Flirted and offered to go for a drive for no particular reason. So there were signs she liked me. Fascinated by the DJ and would always congregate with him and their friends all night. Hated it, being left out. My outlook one of carelessness. Disillusioned, dejected, despondent, and desperate. Why don't I just go and twat him? Cause a raucous. Making sneering, nasty remarks and be told unbecoming of me. That was a revelation. A kind of inference there must be some good in me. Not all bad then. The first half-hearted inverse unintended compliment ever received. I'll take it as a positive.

Tracy was looking after the pub while the landlord away over the weekend. A Saturday night. She had worked behind the bar for several years and was close friends with the landlady. Therefore, trusted to be resident manager for the weekend. It came to closing time and I could see a guy who appeared to be particularly friendly with Tracy, to my dis-like. He wasn't leaving. Feeling uncomfortable and agitated. Hoping that he wasn't what I thought he was. Her boyfriend, or someone of that ilk. The later it got, people would leave but he would remain. The momentum of distress increased materially. The time was going to come when I would have to discover who he was and what he wanted. But having no right over her, weren't even seeing each other. But in my head had reserved her for us. Convinced she and I were going to be together soon. It's just a case of time. The atmosphere changed. One of hostility: eerie silence. Who would speak first? How would it be resolved? There seemed nowhere to go spiritually. I doubted he was going home then and occurred, also staying the night, which compounded despair further. The thought of exclusion, dismissed, and ultimately rejected was unacceptable. That was a no-no. It wasn't long before there were only the three of us. Two in the morning; the lock-in had expired. All had departed but me, the guy, and Tracy. A pacifist: unbecoming to exert aggression or become violent. The eruptions and rumblings would lead me to that desire but ultimately in conflict with the essence of who I am. The apex of the scenario would present itself. Void of dialogue or acknowledgement all night. But he knew I was lingering and hovering, knowing unwelcome. All my rage, despair, self-loathing, hate, grief, pain, and hurt would culminate and accumulate in this very moment. Which way would it go? A fight? An altercation? An exchange of obscenities and profanities?

Threatening language was directed at me to suggest if to stand my ground then it was going to get ugly. The physical reality of the situation became the proof in this illogical drama. She obviously had invited and wanted him there. Choosing him, not me. The notion that there might be something between us was no more than a fantasy. Absent tangible words had never been exchanged to substantiate my claim. Flawed evidence. Led astray by my own insecurities, self-doubts, missing companion, or single human being to mirror my humanity. My mind had deceived into what it wanted to believe. Walked out. Made my way home. By the time departed the pub and got to the street, it hit me. Unsurprisingly, almost anticipated. As though I knew and un-shockable, prophesied in a dream. Shaking, trembling, and shivering. Ironically, into shock. My thoughts changed to a rebellious, carelessness. Absent tears. Hadn't cried since five years old. But an obvious paradigm state shift. Once across the street noting a group of teenagers surrounding a car, at each wheel, the boot, bonnet, and the doors. Seemingly breaking in. They pretended to turn their back to the wall, with impunity. As though they all conveniently needed the toilet instantaneously.

"Carry on boys!" I shouted.

The house was empty. Parents away at the caravan. Josh had bought his own house and Paul had moved out several years prior. We still had milk bottles then. An impulse to put my fist through a window. An overwhelming urge to interpret the emotional pain and distress endured. Picking up an empty milk bottle that happened to be standing there innocently. Began punching the bottle side-on with my fist as hard as possible. After several attempts it wouldn't break. Plan B would be to smash it in the sink, pick a shard of glass, and start slashing my arm and back of hand. Undesirable to dress the wound or clot the bleeding. Merciless.

A sleepless night followed. Traumatised, shaking, and shivering all night long. The next day I'd go back down to the local pub. Still without dressing or plasters. Blood still seeping from the wounds. One of the acquaintances would note:

"What have you done there Jack?"

Before I was able to answer, Josh had retorted:
"He's a f****ing idiot!"

The landlord in our presence. An attempt to console by describing the events of the night before. Before I could finish, Josh had lambasted me yet again:

"We don't want to know any of that, shut your f***ing gob!"

The aggregated omission of care and love had impacted my personal duty of care to the extent daily life would continue as normal. The following Monday at the course premises as usual. Still wounded. Open wounds left unattended. Blood seeping for all to see. Ignorant or in denial of the state presented. Still distraught, trembling, and perplexed. On Mother's return I'd be met with:

"What have you done that for?"

An appointment to see the GP was made. Informed of my symptoms. The diagnosis was nervous breakdown. Prescribed anti-depressants and recommended counselling. In the interim period, defunct and redundant. Still shaking, palpitations, panic attacks, and anxiety. An inability to function. Daily tasks like having a shower or putting the kettle on were major events which appeared too great to bear. A vacuum of knowledge or understanding. But worse than that, they would repudiate what had taken place or what had contributed to it. All in denial. Taboo. The course had come to a natural conclusion and so did the placement, evidently. Unmotivated, void of energy, and life seemingly futile. Rendering me a 'cabbage'. A walking corpse. Physically, mentally, and emotionally disturbed. Lost, confused, distraught, traumatised, overwhelmed, unable to cope or function.

Since Josh's attempted suicide three years prior. Mother had become a born again Christian, through a friend. She was now a regular churchgoer and still in touch with the friend, a Christian Counselling Supervisor. It was suggested I get in touch, the counselling via the Church and circumventing the normal channels of GP. The phone call difficult in itself. Hadn't realised the extent of what had taken place. The inability to perform everyday tasks. The oppression and depression didn't want me to speak to anyone. If I could just lay on my bed and sleep forever, that would work. An offer of male or female was offered. An obvious choice given that men had had such a negative demonstrable effect. Women appeared more receptive, understanding, sympathetic, and engaging. The outcome of this conversation that two women assigned for two sessions per week initially, to be reviewed and revised. Ostensibly, both friends and known each other for years, had spent time at university together. Close and well acquainted. Both Christian. The 'happy-clappy', charismatic, 'do-gooder' type. Informed that Liz was the counsellor and Liza the understudy, observing and gaining experience after a short counselling course. Although Liz was no practised veteran of the subject. She too had only done the six-week fast-track Christian counselling course, in-house.

"We can do anything through Christ who strengthens us!" they would recite.

"Through God all things are possible!" routinely trotted out.

Their disposition was one of nonchalant and blasé. Unknown territory, a one-to-one with anyone was an alien phenomenon. To have not one, but two people's attention uninterrupted, without music, TV, phone or any other distraction was incredible. This was a first. The little knowledge of counselling known was that sessions are agreed from the beginning. The frequency, duration, beginnings, and endings. So the client always knows where they are. This is particularly key and essence to the fundamentals of counselling. Paramount as many conflicts emanate from relationships. Whereby attachment, security, reassurance, safety, and trust are the ultimate objectives. Sacrosanct within the counselling environment to engender this rule or guidance. A duty of care bestowed upon the provider to adhere to these regulations.

They were "Praise the Lord, Hallelujah!", jovial, joyous, super, fantastic, positively glass-full people. The attitude and sentiment from the beginning was reducing sessions, promoting independence, moving on, looking ahead, and leaving all the negatives behind. Making it abundantly clear the views they held about God, the Church, and Christianity. It was suggested I attend church even if it was to get out of the house to confront my anxieties and hear the Word. Unemployed, dis-engaged from higher education or training, it seemed common sense to comply and attend. What had I to lose? Sitting at the very back. Seemingly safe and fitting. Unnoticed. An inability to worship, sing, raise arms, or speak. The meeting would end and the congregation would chatter, have coffee and fellowship with other members. Body language austere, awkward, and agitated. My posture distant and alienated. Unable to connect with anyone. Unsightly, that a vacant bystander would approach or dare to connect with this ominous stoic figure. The counsellors' would pick up on this point in the next session. Expressing that my social skills need some attention. That I need to start talking to people. Unsupported without guidance, reassurance, or a platform to practise. If missing introductions or invitations offered to a social gathering or inclusion in events, how the hell is it going to happen? A month in, familiar with behaviours, attitudes, and personalities. The exception being void of personality. Digressing into private conversations about their personal lives during the session. Only resuming when the discourse had exhausted itself. Liza had recently given birth and thought it acceptable to bring the baby-carrier—with baby—I hasten to add. Dumping it at my feet as an inconvenient intruder and obstacle. In spite of the fantasy of uninterrupted attention while revealing my deepest pain, loss, and grief. A plethora of interruptions would disrupt the ideal. Random people walking straight in to the room. The security buzzer ringing regularly from the ground-floor main entrance. The phone would ring, and noises could be heard from the adjoining room. Six months had elapsed unchanged. Unstable at best. Liz would ask me to describe my circumstances.

"Emotionally disturbed!" I replied.
"Oh no, I don't think you are that. That's a bit extreme," she quipped.

Dismissive of my very well discerning, intelligent mind. Then she would enquire:

"How do you feel?" she queried.
"I feel ostracised!" said innocently.

She came down heavy on me.

"What do you mean ostracised? You can't be ostracised! You have got to be ostracised by somebody!"

Absolutely 'friggin' clueless, came the responsive thought.

On another occasion I mentioned:
"If I could just do xyz...then I'll be able to cope."

The response was a glib, flippant,

"But God doesn't want you to cope!"

There were still urges and a propensity to self-harm. You can't live a life like that and automatically step into a new skin. It was going to take time to build a foundation, self-esteem, to like and ultimately love myself. They didn't help matters. Instituting a method of support going forward in that we wouldn't have confirmed regular appointments. So that I would know where I stood in terms of being able to voice my despair: consoled and reassured. No, apparently now I had to call the counselling office and they would make an appointment. It was a farce. Weeks before I got a reply, then it could be another two weeks if not more post that. Unreliable and undependable. Too busy contributing to cosmetic church work, youth groups, preparing the next sermon or religious meeting. Fabricating textiles to make the place look pretty and flower-arranging. No guarantee if or when I would see them. Ignorant to the reality of my plight. Didn't have the capacity or comprehension to accept when I didn't talk to them I didn't talk to anyone. The period were apart I have to harbour, and retain the events. Disappointments, struggles, despair, excruciating anxiety, paranoia, self-loathing and reclusive lifestyle. Absent of a single human being to turn to. The GP's are uninterested. Family are aloof, distant, and in denial. But never had time regardless. The intention on their part was to gradually wean me off counselling, dependency, and release me back into the world I had come from. Motivating me to do something positive with my life. Start a course or get a job.

"You can't sit at home everyday!" they'd say.

Fortunately, it didn't take much effort to discover an opportunity in the local press. A checker at a local dairy distribution depot. Four hours per day, four in the morning till eight. The job description was to record the quantity of milk and dairy products the milk-men would opt to load their vehicles with. A spate of theft, fraud, and deceit had taken place in their recent history. The catalyst for taking on new employees to quell, if not extinguish, the amount of milk disappearing on a daily basis. Already equipped with CCTV cameras on the bay. But insufficient to identify the culprits, methods, and collate evidence of who, where, and when. My previous stint as a milkman would stand me in good stead. Also, in an ironic way, the fiddling at Baxters, subsequently being found out and sacked would actually be my saving grace. The fact I am shrewd, insightful, open-minded and don't suffer fools gladly. The perfect candidate. Similarly, a good 'copper' is one that has life experience. Did take the sweets from the local shop, ride his bike without lights, and indulge in the anti-social fraternity with his or her immediate contemporaries.

Inconceivable the work would overwhelm despite my state. No matter how difficult it would appear, soldier on. Unabated anxiety, stress, palpitations, panic attacks, and chronic chest pain. Far from abated. Actually full-blown traumatised, emotionally disturbed, hysterical, unable to live in my own skin, constant panic. Notwithstanding paranoia, depressed and inanimate. A prime target for verbal abuse, insults, mocking and berating. Another example of working-class, poorly educated, stereotypical South Yorkshire men.

In spite of the aforementioned burdens, absent inhibitions when it came to exerting my authority, scrutinising every concealment, cavity, and intention to deceive. The approach was rigorous, disciplined, and methodical. Paying dividends. Becoming a regular occurrence to detect, identify, and prove the misconduct at hand. Frequent violent objections, retaliations, gesticulations, and blame apportioned. My fault they were stealing and had been caught red-handed. A complete revolt and rebuke of responsibility or acceptance of crime. Some would threaten to 'smack' or do me over. Called all the usual expletives and profanities. The disposition and demeanour unfavourable. Pensive, angst, weak, vulnerable, exposed, and defunct. Addressed as 'smiler'. Sarcastic, condescending, and derogatory comments would make the day. My determination to continue and succeed was unfettered by their own ignorance: lack of intelligence and understanding. Six months had been committed to this role. The ability to manage and cope would peak at four hours. Although failing to manage or cope, but suffered. The subliminal and historical drivers were still rooted. A desire to get-on, achieve, and aspire. The hope one day to be a 'somebody'. To advance, grow, improve, and ultimately excel. Another dichotomous ambivalent scenario presented. Logical and normal thinking would suggest: Don't even do the milk job but give it all up. Stay at home. Rest, recover, self-improve and maybe even love yourself. Allow yourself to be kind and justify the deserving love and care. But the counter-argument to press forward, soldier on, deny oneself, advance, and move up the ladder of life. The zeal, ambition, and drive of my root, the real Jack, would stymie the former thought process. Which force would win the day? Would the dire health, pain, failing, anxiety, hopelessness and helplessness, the absent social skills, self-doubt, and a nullified esteem triumph? Or would my 'will' supersede any afflictions and adversity. Overcome the battlefield that lay before me.

Mum and Dad were besotted by the dog. It would receive preferential treatment. Spoken to and greeted on a daily basis. Walked twice per day: treats, haircuts, washes, toys, cuddles, and conversation. This would play out in front of me. Unrecognised in my state. Oblivious to my daily struggles, pains, torment, panic, and fear. Wash-rinse-repeat with Sandy and revere him as prime focus. I'd be expected to take him out for walks and do the same in their absence. I hated the bloody thing. The inference that the dog was obviously more important than me. Thinking about that very point for a moment. A dog is worth more than me. Overlooked, ignored, rejected, and unidentifiable. Circumventing around me. The sanctuary more precious than ever as the enduring environment would take its toll. The compulsion or religious aspect would prompt me to return daily. To escape, decrypt the encrypted messy thoughts, and yield some solace.

An inability to cry had been conditioned, learned, and honed from the formative years. The instruction to "Stop crying!" ignored, unattended to, and abandoned would reinforce this belief. Any painful, disappointing hurtful experience numbed and dumbed down, suppressed, and denied. For some unknown reason prompted and motivated to seek out some old family holiday photos. Perhaps to make sense of origin, put the pieces of the jigsaw together. Discover a meaning and purpose, resolve, clarity, transparency, and ultimate conclusion. After rifling through dozens of albums of summer holidays of bygone years, one particular photo stood out among the rest. Distinct and stark. I picked it up and held it before my eyes, staring intently; transfixed. Within seconds it hit home. I knew this was it. This ironically was what I didn't want to discover. The truth. Instantaneously, something changed, spiritually and chemically. Trauma set in, trembling, shaking and shivering, grief stricken, overwhelmed with emotion, unable to cry. The photograph was of Dad, Josh, Paul, and me. A dad with his three boys on a family holiday. The focal point being and the cross-hairs of contention. The patently clear, obvious separation and distance between us all. We were literally feet apart. Void of physical attachment or connection. Aloof and individually separate. This was a bolt of lightning to my world. The confirmation, proof, and validation that Dad wasn't a dad. It was representative and symbolic of many other roles and responsibilities. Emblematic of being unloved, untouched, uncared for, missing connection, attachment and unknown personally. The trauma would pervade unabated for the rest of that day. Distraught, overwhelmed, unable to tell anyone what had been seen and experienced. Fortunately, a Saturday afternoon. A church meeting the next day, Sunday. Liz present and hopefully could receive some prayer and spiritual support. A hugely significant event, and wouldn't come to terms with it easily. On passing Dad in the kitchen, the closer I'd get the more intense and overwhelmed. On sitting at the dinner-table; only feet away becoming unbearable, agitated, disturbed, shaking and trembling inside. Unable to say a word. Maintaining this state for another eighteen hours until the time came to go to church the following morning.

As predicted, woke up the following morning, as I had gone to bed, pre-empting the meeting ahead, sensing the whole world on my shoulders. Heavily burdened, carrying a weight beyond my ability to sustain. As was usual at a meeting, an inability to worship, sing, or express adoration and praise. Sat, arms folded, mute, and incapacitated. My main focus to tell Liz after the meeting what I'd seen and experienced. Seeking her out in the mêlée of the congregation chattering upon closure of the meeting.

"Liz, I've got something to tell you," I would utter softly and quietly, punctuated with trembling.

"Yes, what is it?" she said concerned.
Silent pause.
The words didn't come out. An unordered, distorted, mumbling and stuttering did, indecipherable.
She didn't get it. A concerned frown lay across her face. I'd try again.

"I saw something yesterday!"

"Yes, what was it?" she replied a second time.

By this time breaking down. The words would never leave my mouth. Once it started coming that was it. Similarly to the Hoover Dam breaching its wall. A flood of tears would follow. Emotion, grief, despair, loss, pain, sorrow, mixed and fused together. Inconsolable and uncontrollable. Incessant and relentlessly. Within the next thirty minutes the majority of people had vacated the premises. Eventually the leadership and elders would sit me down on a chair. Five members laying hands all over me. On my back, head, chest and hands. Over an hour before peace restored and stable enough to return home.

There was an ad in the local paper. A two-year, full-time course at Brooks College, Huddersfield. HND computing. An initial excitement upon digesting the details. Sounds good. A three letter acronym. Rolls off the tongue well. 'HND'. Worth looking into at least. Could apply and see where it got me. A vacuum of A-levels or anything of that ilk, uneducated at school. Only the City and Guilds certificate obtained via the corresponding course. Personally, didn't think it was worth the paper written on. Little or no respect from the education or business world in terms of being a substantial and comprehensive course of high calibre. The beginning of the beginning. An introduction to the introduction. The application went through, and to my utter amazement an interview was arranged to discuss capability. Whether I had the available resources, intellect and attitude to complete the course. The proverbial stress, anticipation, pre-empting every eventuality before it happened. Hyper-vigilant to the max. Priming for the scrutiny, questioning, and the possibility of my shame and badness being exposed or revealed unwittingly.

The day arrived all systems go, 'Def-con five'. Unaware which building, entrance, or department. Signs and notices intimidating. Alien to their culture or environment. 'Faculty', 'Atrium', 'Campus', 'Undergrad', 'Postgrad'. The anxiety would kick in unaware of the root cause or source. Could be the 'being late punctuality phobia', approval addiction obsession, inept, incompetent, feeble, weak, and unqualified. That I shouldn't even be contemplating such a venture. Wholly inappropriate and only for bright, privileged, competently educated and intelligent candidates, please. Sensing a fraud. Unwelcome. Out of my depth: deceptive and peddling a lie. My suspicions, cynicism and self-preservation. The reliable unfaltering intelligence proved good yet again. It wasn't to be. After much distress, panic, and fear of being late, not finding the right location in time and being prepared for the interview. The interviewer went AWOL. No show. Missed appointment. That was it. Obviously a sign. Confirmation that it wasn't for me. Read it wrong. Tried too hard. Aiming to be a somebody when it was not destined. It's not going to happen. The journey home was an arduous one. Feeling dejected, despondent, disillusioned, and disappointed. My mind on a mission to discern and discover the true reason for his absence. Objectively, it could have been an oversight, an error of judgement, maybe a mistake. The unlikely chance there had been a communication problem somewhere along the lines. My details had genuinely been misplaced or unwittingly ignored. Subjectively, the purpose and intent from the powers and principalities of hell would orchestrate this scenario for my ultimate demise: devastation and destruction. Convincing me of my worthless, purposeless life. Invalidated, dis-approved, and rejected again. So they wouldn't have to depend on their imps and minions. Capable of destroying myself without coercion, persuasion, and suggestive thinking on their part. The only way to reveal the truth to discover and learn of the facts. That would require a telephone call to the admissions department to clarify what went wrong. Simples. With great hesitation that my concerns and doubts realised, I took the almighty step of calling them. To acquire the pertinent contact details of the incumbent. What can he say? They're full up? Occupied? Unqualified? I'd never make it?

Dismayed and aghast. He was full of apologies. Screwed up, cocked up, and lost it.
Game on. To cut to the chase, it resulted in a two-minute conversation, what did I know, topics and concepts studied prior, and did I have what it took to do a full-time course.

"Yes, of course I can, no problem!" responded promptly.

Done deal!

"Okay then I'll accept you on that basis," the interviewer confirmed.

A surreal moment of surprise, astonishment and almost giddiness attached to a private wry smile. Tempered by going it alone again. Family, unknowing, uncaring, ignorant of academia, higher education, aspirations, or social mobility. My current thinking was to continue with the milk job, four in the morning till eight, call home for breakfast and a drink, then thirty-minute drive to college in the centre of Huddersfield. That way, I wouldn't get into debt via student loans: could pay my own way and keep the car running.

THE WILDERNESS

The night before enrolment I'd be primed and pre-emptive. Excited, fused with fear, anxiety, and the the proverbial anticipatory reticence and self-doubt. The only recce had been the 'no show' from the interviewer. That location I knew, but not the enrolment department. The level of distress and untenable ability to hold it together wasn't strictly correlated to the enrolment. It had become a regular, familiar facet to my well-being. A daily dose of being perplexed, pensive, incapacitated, hyper-vigilant, and an inability to cope with day-to-day life. This was normal. Worried, if I would find the correct place to enrol. Concerned of my ability to speak. The overwhelming fear of being seen, spiritually. Would they see my shame? Would they know I knew what they knew? Still feeling a fraud. The irrational, paranoid, illogical unhelpful thinking would win the day. Walking from the car in the general direction of the college was enough to turn me back. The people walking in opposition down the street became like grains in a sand storm, a flake within a blizzard or white-out. Too many, too fast. Invasive, intrusive, threatening, so that it could consume me at any second. A battle of the mind would ensue. A test of the will to override the psychological war that appeared so real. Turn back. It's too much! Go to a safe place, a refuge. Don't run into the storm. Run away from it.

I continued. Chronic chest pain, palpitations and panic. As though my heart was going to jump out of my chest. I arrived at the main building but no sign of enrolment. Confused and lost, observing and monitoring for a glimpse of a sign. I'd have to ask someone. It proved right again. The look on their faces said it all. 'Strange'. A concerned frown and eyes that decrypted me as 'troubled soul'. I'd have to walk the fifty yards down the street to another building, which was the designated spot for my particular course. A major upheaval and disruption to my thinking, which would have liked itineraries, plans, locations, and times to be set in stone, and definite. However, the location was eventually reached. Proof of identity, evidence of address, filling out forms and confirming a few details. That was it. Enrolled. The experience had taken its toll and glad to be returning home for some temporary solace.

Continuing with the original intention of continuing to work on the milk job while attending college five days per week. Leave work at eight, quick breakfast, then drive down the M1 to college for 9:00 a.m start. The first day unnerving. What would the other students be like? Would I be the dumb ass of the class? Would they have done A-levels, had a good upbringing, or had teachers as parents, or just generally more advanced than me? Once entering the class I found a seat which, by coincidence, happened to be next to Maria. Little did I realise till later what dark secrets we might share. The incredible probability that the girl sitting next to me on my first day had first-hand experience of abuse, trauma, anxiety, fear, and paranoia. We hit it off immediately. Surreal. Unprecedented to hit it off with anyone. To share banter, trivial conversation, deep complex emotional problems and a shared suffering was unbelievable. Instantly friends. Kindered spirits. Despite her being married and having a young daughter. We were class mates. It seemed the logical thing to do at lunch time. To go out together and share views, opinions about the tutor, other students, and our first-day experience. Apparent how identical our journey's had been. A mutual gratitude for meeting each other. An unintended blessing and support by pure circumstance. A serendipitous encounter. Sharing our mutual foibles and idiosyncrasies. Flaws, weaknesses, vulnerabilities, and little behaviours we'd retained, to reassure and comfort in our distress. Cling and hold both thumbs in the palm of your hand; on each hand. We would ultimately counsel each other unwittingly. A mutual strength of support, as and when needed. It made college life more interesting, bearable, and to spend most days with your best friend was great. Her mother had attempted to kill her and her sister. She was now sectioned in an institution. Maria had been brought up in care, and like me, was struggling to hold it together.

It wasn't plain sailing at college. Most concepts were difficult. The absence and lack of educational attainment in all subjects would hinder the progress. A case of learning on the fly. Picking it up as I went along. That equated to trial and error: getting it wrong, making a mistake, learning how not to do it. Then, slowly but surely would get it right. My grammar and literacy had been historically poor. Having to write reports and theses several thousand words long soon gave me the practice and confidence to go on and re-invest this newfound knowledge onto other projects and experiences.

A month into the first semester, my health was significantly deteriorating. Unable to sleep. Living on adrenaline. Struggling to cope with the milk job, the responsibility, pressure, and the hostile environment. On arrival home daily, I'd walk straight through the house, switch the kettle on, and before I had removed my coat the computer was switched on. My former regimes of superior discipline, righteousness, punctuality, and the desire to please. Commencement of homework the very same day was bestowed to me. I would automatically sit down at the computer missing rest or relaxation and continue working. To add to the aforementioned symptoms, I would feel tearful, depressed, shaking and trembling to the point when enough was enough. Another appointment was made for the GP. He told me explicitly:

"Give up the day job! You're suffering from fatigue by doing too much. Take a break!"

That's what I did. Financially, grants and loans were available. I could manage while living at home. The desire to succeed and be a somebody, would manifest itself though my study. A Pass or Merit was insufficient. Every grade had to be a Distinction. I would move hell and high-water to get a 'D'. Non-conducive to loving myself or being kind and caring. More of a punishing, persecuting, approval addiction aspiration. To be validated, accepted, approved of, seen and liked.

The body language and persona were dire. The inability to look up. Embarrassed by own existence as standard. Stoic, inanimate, and pensive. Fearful, vulnerable and feeble. The slightest iota of attention would flush my face bright red with shame. The approach to the classroom each morning, pausing pending entry. A deep breath, compose oneself, talk to self, and enter. My failing social skills, if any. An utterance of a few mumbled, softly spoken words for speech.

A preponderance of presentations was a prerequisite and mandatory to partake. An awful degrading experience. One that could not be avoided. The social dimension alone was enough to render me stuttering, stammering, glowing bright red, aware they knew what I knew, which compounded and perpetuated the suffering further. Elated when it was all over until the next one would arrive. My monotonous, quiet, soft voice endeavouring to convince, educate, and inform through presentation skills.

The refectory at break and lunchtimes another zone that would render me overwhelmed. Five other of my course students sat around the table, the place full of other tutors, staff, and students from other courses. The conversations were always difficult to enter. Invariably off topic. Areas I couldn't deal with. About sex, relationships, girlfriends, and family. I would close up and shutdown. My coping mechanism was to leave the room. Go for a walk and stand at the door of the main entrance, inhale fresh air to quell the heat and perspiration generated through this social jungle.

The choice had been made to channel and direct my negative energy into the study. It was a win-win. The frustration, inner rage, despair, and anger could be used for good. It seemed to work. Success and distinctions were coming one after the other. However euphoric, jubilant, or exuberant my spirit would yield, a cavity of known contemporaries, friends, family or mutual acquaintances that could share my short-lived joy. The success wouldn't be mirrored back to me; confirmed, approved, validated, or accepted. My colleagues would ring their mums, dads, girlfriends and boyfriends to share the moment of achievement. Standing there envying that rare experience that only others would appreciate. My submissions were never late nor substandard, but exemplary.

The sanctuary would never be forsaken nor forgot. A reliable, dependable source of refreshment, consoling, solace, redeeming, and special. Called to action as and when required, always awaiting my next rendezvous. Some days at college were just untenable. Depending how my health would manifest that day or the pressures set before me; a module deadline, presentation, assessment, or group work. The overwhelming anxiety, panic-attacks, the inability to cope, would see me fleeing to safer climbs. Some days, two hours were the threshold. Other days three or four could be endured before having to succumb to the agitation and flee the immediate environment.

Josh hadn't changed over the years. You might think as you grow older and mature the quarrels, hostility, conflicts, and differing views would stay in the past. But no: as ever, belligerent, abrasive, failing in eye contact or acknowledgement. If we happened to be in the same environment, more often than not Mum's house, we would pass each other, disengaged. Unlike me, had worked constantly and consistently at Baxters, bought his own house and lived there with current girlfriend. But on this occasion we both found ourselves at Mum's. He must have called in to drop something off. I was having tea; about six in the evening.

Trivial and innocuous words were exchanged. Disagreeing on the minutiae of the issue at hand. Suddenly out of the blue he exploded into a bout of rage, cursing, slander, verbally abusive, insults, degrading, derogatory, denigrating, and disparaging language.

"You're an awful nasty person!"
"You'll never have a girlfriend or friends!"
"I hate you!"
"You'll always be on your own, you sad bastard!"

Mother would stand there in the midst; silent. Unwilling to do the right thing and stop it. Unwittingly condoning the act that had just occurred. Almost in agreement, justifying and believing every word he had launched. Unbearable. The emotional pain, despair, self-loathing compounded by my own self-hatred, culminated in exiting the room, breaking down, running upstairs to my room, searching for a razor blade in my draw and slashing the back of my hand multiple times. Traumatised, trembling, shaking, crying and devastated. In the midst of horrifying days, losing the will to live. Undesirable to live this hellish life any longer. How someone—your own brother—can do this. A common occurrence at the sanctuary, I'd be suicidal. Contorted in despair. The warring factions of,'don't want to live this life anymore'. To, what if? What if I fall in love, meet a beautiful woman, get married and have kids? What if I do it now and miss out on all that?

A deficiency of on-going support. In fact, annulled support. Fobbed off, denied, rebuffed, and dismissed. By all the stakeholders. The churchgoers would pray and abandon.

"Praise the Lord. Hallelujah!"
"We can't do it for you. There's only you that can do it!" commonly heard.

Mother was clueless, her own mother had had a breakdown too, but hadn't gleaned anything of use to minister. Lived on worry and anxiety. Neurotic with a tendency to avoid, escape, and deny any problematic situation. Dad was in a world of his own and had never personally acknowledged me all my life. Josh and Paul lived their own lives. Liz and Liza more concerned about the next church meeting, youth work, religious duties, drama, evangelism, flower-arranging and general church life tittle-tattle. The GP refusing to maintain eye contact, typing up his notes, handing me another script for anti-depressants. Attending college the following day though uneventful. Hand undressed, gashes and gaping wounds for all to see.

Maintaining an unorthodox connection to the few Christians that were known. Primarily via proxy. Associated with Mother through the cell group, or acquaintances of Liz and Liza that were casually introduced. It wasn't a choice to go to church. The only lifeline; the alternative to continue in my withdrawn, reclusive state. Although still mute at the cell group and in the church meetings. Body language ominous, obverse, and incongruous, missing a singular human being who would look at me, never mind greet, accept, and engage. The visual signs of togetherness, family, unity, and community would only fuel the fury within. Rejection had always been my Achilles heel. To see two together, arm in arm, hand in hand. Bonding, relating, affectionate and loving would send my core emotional indicator to 'Def-con five'; off the scale. A propensity to self-harm; quelling the overwhelming pain. In spite of being surrounded by a Christian community and church my paradoxical sense of self wouldn't succumb to pressure, in the midst of storms, giants, waves, holocausts, and harrowing events. I knew my mind. Disallowed to coerce, persuade, influence, or exploit my evident vulnerability. The little spiritual nous or philosophy attained; that things happen for a reason. If phenomena or alchemy would immerse my life in a positive redeeming way, then would gladly embrace and not rebuke. If good would come from this journey and experience then it couldn't be all that bad.

I always felt out of it. Unlike other Christians. Inconceivable to walk about spouting and espousing "Praise the Lord!", "Hallelujah!", "God is good!", or "God can do all things." My state incapable of raising arms, waving hands in worship. Muted didn't lend itself to praise or exaltation and in fine song. Prayer out of the question. An inability to connect with any living phenomenon, including God. The worst Christian walking this earth. But continuing in daily life, driving to and from college, church and back. There were signs: a billboard with a metaphor. As though someone talking to me. Then dismissing it as pure co-incidence. A few days later another sign on the radio: another on the TV. The overall conclusion that it was beyond reasonable doubt. The philosophy was good. I'm being wooed not by Christians but by God himself. A relating had begun between the Almighty and me. A private, uninterrupted dialogue. The penny dropped. I'm being called. He wants me. He wants me to go the whole hog. Not about attending church. But to relinquish and capitulate. Surrender all. Come to Him. To accept Jesus in my life as Lord and Saviour; over all of my life. Whoa!! Wowswers! But how do I go about it? I can't recognise you exist. With an incapacity to bond, defunct, bound in bondage with walls, defences, shells, camouflage, and riot gear. Who will penetrate whom?

Liz had suggested a Sunday evening church meeting that I might like to attend. Led by a group of young guys from a Bible College; relatively close to Sheffield. Noting they often had a word from God. Intriguing one thought. A word from God. Wow! I was that desperate; all else was ineffective. What had I to lose? An urgency to get out more anyway. But more than that, an urge to yell, scream, and express was the motivating factor. The following Sunday 11 Feb 1996 I would give it a go. Unhappy, burdened with pain, angry, agitated, and hated people. The more liberated and free the congregation were, the more angry I became. The worship, joyful singing, clapping and praising God would irritate and provoke my inner demons. Arms crossed, the only one in the whole building sat down. Intransigent. Locked in and shutdown. The frustration of being mute, bound, and incapacitated manifested in my thoughts. Visions of going ballistic, smashing the very chair I was sat on. Over and over again. Launching, smashing, destroying, tearing, ripping at anything and everything in sight in an act of wanton vandalism. My face glowing bright red with rage and despair. Re-living the very real experience through my imagination. Cursing the environment, setup, farce, and whole meeting. Expletives and obscenities would fly through my mind at speed. And then as the crescendo reached its climax of intensity, seconds away from implementing my forethought and rehearsal of ultimate destruction, I looked up. Unbeknown the worship leader had been waiting on God. Pacing from left to right on the stage and pulpit area. Deep in thought and meditation as he patiently waited for the Word to come. Suddenly looked up. Stared intently towards me, right into my eyes. Discovered. No! Get away from me, my instincts responded. Looking immediately away; towards the floor. You didn't see me; carry on.

Refusing to alter his gaze but kept eyes transfixed the whole time. I've been seen. The next moment I heard over the microphone.

"Church! God is speaking to me about this young man here!"
He came off the stage right down to my chair and stood by me.

"I don't know if you are a Christian but God is talking to me about you right now" he said.
By this time I had broken down, crying and sobbing, overwhelmed at the spectacle, timing, events and the momentous occasion of being seen.

“No, I’m not!” I replied.

This was the moment I had been waiting for.

“If you would like to give your life to Jesus and grant him the right to be Lord and Saviour over all of your life and accept Him into your life then we will do it.”

A resolute affirmation, “Yes!, I wanted to.”

He would come to me the moment the meeting had been brought to closure. An abundance of noise could be heard, chitter-chatter from the attendees, background music still playing, the sound of chairs being pushed along the floor, and general frenetic activity following a meeting. He would present and recite scriptures to me from the Bible and then instructed me to repeat the words he would say.

The content irrelevant. Having said anything to redeem myself, to extricate from the hell that had become the norm. The words were muffled, indecipherable, cryptic, and barely audible. Repeating what I thought I heard, but all the while thinking, surely this has to be specific? Insufficient to ramble, stutter, and stumble a few words out. The words were with authority, reverent, emblematic, venerable, laudable, eminent, regal and held power in the spiritual realms. Surely you had to say the specific word to get the required outcome? Reciting Cod, the Devil and I was never going to cut it; or Cod works in mysterious ways. The actual words that did eventually leave my mouth were stuttered, stumbled, rambled upon and pitifully uttered. The shock of the evening; in awe and overwhelmed at the spectacle. Informing he would write to me in the following days and had a word from God for me.

A dearth of community support. A vacuous nurture group for new born-again Christians. Leaders, pastoral and elders nowhere to be seen or heard. The ‘Spouters’ and ‘espousers’ long gone. Purported senior long-standing ministers of God too busy. That was it. Left to it. Inadequately prepared, ill equipped, dumbfounded, lost and confused. Unknowing where or how to read the Bible. Ignorant of how to strike up a conversation with God. Would He listen or would He reply if He did listen? A bitter sweet moment. Elated that I'd reached that point. But disillusioned and disappointed by the appropriate support needed to enter the conversation with God. The only hope was the pending, imminent letter: 'A Word from God'.

Word for Jack Jones – 11/2/96

I really believe the Lord is saying to me to tell you He's not playing games. God is not playing games. That He loves you and He's chosen you. And He wants you to know you've got the real thing. It's not a fake. He loves you. And it's a love like you've never had before. It's going to make you steadfast and it's going to make you secure. And you're not going to have to prove yourself anymore. I believe God has got his hand on your life in a unique way. It is time to stop running. There is no more abandonment. He loves you. He loves you. He is not promising you a bed of roses, nor is he promising an easy time. But He is promising you his *friendship and His love. He's promising you a relationship that you can hold on to.*

In spite of feeling fraudulent, ill-equipped, incapable, and unqualified to be a Christian, the least I could do was attend church meetings. How else would the conversation with God develop? Requiring the presence of both parties to accommodate 'the conversation'. The prevailing symptoms, traits, quirks, and behaviours were still intact. Mentally, emotionally, and socially little had changed in nearly eighteen months of seeing Liz and Liza. They had kept and maintained my status quo or modus operandi. But failing in progress. Static and immutable.

The word had got around that a 'big-hitter' was coming to town. This translated to a Prophetic Minister with a commendable reputation visiting our Church in the coming weeks; a big event not to be missed. Superfluous to my thinking, ignorant of what prophecy was or how an ordinary human being could possess paranormal or supernatural powers to foresee the future. The cynical side of me paid it little attention. Too lost and bewildered in my wilderness to be adept and astute in religious spiritual matters.

The incumbents responsible: seniors, teachers, relatives, parents, and guardians had reneged on their duty. Other than attending college, investing all my energy into the assignments; seeking refuge and solace at the sanctuary. Whereby the regular three-mile jog, circumventing the whole reservoir would sustain me for another few days: and attending a random counselling session. Essentially a recluse. Dissociative at evenings and weekends; withdrawn and closed. The tipping factor in deciding to attend was essentially born out of frustration and despair of inhumanity. The excruciating loneliness and isolation of exposed to a social environment but feeling dis-connected and solitary. A vain attempt to think, 'If I'm around people it will quell or console my spirit.' The downside on arrival was the anxiety, palpitations, fear, and trepidation. What if they worship? I don't do 'happy-clappy'. It's going to be a difficult night, but I'll persevere. One of the leadership team would attempt to engage over a cup of coffee. The shame overwhelming. Voice barely audible, face bright red with embarrassment. Feeling bad at the prospect of identified or discovered. The time had come for the speaker and Prophet to begin. Unaware of how these events proceed. Void of preconceptions but an open mind. Evident he would select members of the congregation at random. Ostensibly, who he deemed God had informed him to elect. Thirty minutes in, four people selected, invited up onto the stage and spoke over them in front of the whole congregation. Recorded and transcribed later. Unbeknown Liz and Liza must have arrived late and sitting at the back. The Prophet would scan and survey the room. I rarely looked up. Much of my time around college was spent looking towards the floor and in other social scenarios my sight would wander. But a quick glance to observe the next delegate and similarly to a month before, his eyes transfixed on me.

"This young man here please, in the woolly jumper" he requested.

No, not me. I knew the chosen garment was distinctive and heavy as to keep me warm as it had been cold of late. But there must have been others wearing woolly jumpers.

"Yes, you there, son!"
The worst possible outcome.
"Oh shit!"

The fight and flight kicked in. Feeling flushed before I had left my seat. Ba bum ba bum ba bum, went my heart. A catalyst to flee or fly. But there were over a hundred people watching; how can I possibly opt out then?

Prophetic Word for Jack Jones - 20.3.96
Graham Cook

Father, thank you. Jack, God absolutely loves you, absolutely, loves you. Will forgive you anything, anything in the past, right up to the moment I picked you out. Everything going back is forgiven, is forgotten, is under the blood. And God is just saying to you. SON, YOU JUST COME, YOU JUST COME. There is a call upon your life, and has been for a very long time. A call upon your life. God called you Jack. He has called you. Again I saw you with a strong supernatural call upon you. I believe God has called you. This may sound strange but God has called you to fight beasts. He's called you to warfare.

He has called you to be a strong man, full of strength, full of power. Full of Anointing, to stand in the presence of God. He has called you to fight, Jack. He has called you to fight. He has called you to fight. He has called you to fight. He has called you to warfare. He has called you to fight the Demonic. He has called you to fight things. He's called you to break bondages on people he has called you with a sword in your hands to cut chains and shackles and see people set free and delivered, particularly from Demonic things. I see a strong supernatural anointing upon your life that will preach the Gospel, that will see people delivered and set free. I see you again travelling around the world in a team, with a strong

Anointing upon you. I see you speaking in meetings of thousands where the Anointing of God will come upon those people because the Anointing of God is in you. I see people: I see the Holy Spirit moving around auditoriums where you are and I see you laying hands on people and things happening and I see a tremendous move of the Holy Spirit happening around your ministry. But God right now is just shaping you for the future. You are going to be a man of the Word, Jack. Strong in the word, strong in faith. You are always going to have this sense of inadequacy, and that is important, because I believe that the power of God coming through you is going to be huge. And also you will always have this feeling of inadequacy which is good. You should be weak. You should be weak. The best thing in the world is being weak before God, once you just get it sorted in your heart, that the real power belongs to God.

And you are just an unprofitable servant, and you are just like a Gideon, you're just like the weakest people on the earth. Once you get that sorted in your spirit, ministry is dead easy, because everything is down to God and you. You just have to make a start somewhere and see what God will do. And He will always show up and that is going to be the Anointing on your life, because God has called you. He has called you. He does not mind all your doubts, and everything else right now. He doesn't mind all those things, doesn't mind that

You sometimes feel out of it, but now He is just saying SON, there is a calling upon your life and so He is preserving and has preserved your life and will preserve your life. The hand of God is upon you and He is calling you. He is raising you up to be a man of God who has power, supernatural Anointing, but favour with God, favour with God, and He just says to you Son: You are My Son and I'm your Father, I'm your Father Jack, I'm your Father and I won't let you down and I won't leave you and I won't reject you, and I won't walk away from you, because I am your Father and you won't feel orphaned, because I am your Father and you belong to me. And I've always been your Father, always watched over you and will watch over you, because you will be a man with a strong father's Anointing upon him and even as you move in Ministry around the world you will raise up and you will collect many sons. You will disciple many people into the Ministry. Son, the hand of God is upon you and I believe this is a new day, God has just given you a new page and He is saying, Son, we're going to write on this page together, but it's a brand new page, nothing of the past, all statements made against you, God cancels them: all negative things over your life right now, every curse, every negative word spoken over you, by teachers, by teachers, every negative word spoken over you, in family, by people around you, every word you've spoken over yourself, the times when you've said I'm stupid, I'm so stupid. Every negative word right now God breaks the power over it, over your life right now and He says to you Son, YOU ARE MY SON, MY SON, and you are beloved. I call you beloved Jack. You are my Son. This is a new day and a new page and there is nothing on it yet. This prophetic word is the first thing I have written on this page. Let the first words say: Jack. YOU ARE MY SON AND I HAVE CALLED YOU TO BE A MAN OF FAITH, A MAN OF POWER, A MAN WHO IS A WARRIOR AND A FIGHTER, AND I WILL HELP YOU THROUGH ALL THE BATTLES THAT YOU WILL FACE. Every battle is sent by me, allowed by me, Son, to bring you into a fresh understanding of who I am, who I am for you. I will be your Father: I will be your Warrior. I'll fight for you, even as you will fight along side me. There is a high calling of God upon your life, Jack, the High calling of God.

Know that he has chosen you and He has picked you out to belong to him, to stand for Him in these days and in these years. We pray blessing on Him Father, pray blessing on Him Father, may he know what it is to be a Son, May he know what it is to have you as Father in the name of Jesus that the revelation of your fathering be upon Him Father, in Jesus Name.

My response and reaction to hearing this was one of wonderment; bewilderment and incredulity. Poles apart from the contemporary trials and tribulations. Inconceivable and incomprehensible. The disbelief, a complete stranger unknown could have such deeply profound knowledge; not so much of the past but of the future. How on earth did he know I berated, criticised and bullied; in my own head. The curses spoken over me, vacant friends, girlfriend, or success in life.

That I was bad. Why would someone hidden and unseen be projected into the light for all to see when mute, unqualified, anti-social, and redundant. Similarly to Moses and Jeremiah. Oratory isn't within my reach. The multitudes will cause me anxiety. I will stutter, stumble, and fall. The congregation aghast. During the next counselling session expressing their affirmation and revealing beside themselves, sobbing tears on the night.

A few people at Church had got together to arrange a badminton session one evening during the week. Invited, to make small steps to be socially confident and building self-esteem. One of the attendees was Richard. It appeared Richard and Liz were particularly friendly; to my dislike. It would evoke strong emotions of jealousy, anger and rejection. Togetherness had always been an Achilles heel. Viewing two united, while on the periphery would send me over the edge. A trigger that had caused me to previously self-harm. The weak spot. Playing doubles. The rage, anger, and despair overwhelming. Manifest and exhibit through my actions. Every time the shuttlecock would fall in my direction, it would get whacked so hard you would think you were at Wimbledon. Invariably, an audible follow-through "Arrrghhhh!", heard. They must have known, self-evident. The indignant rage, disappointment, frustration, and inability to connect yielding through the racket. Smashing shots with all my strength and power. Far beyond considered normal. Missing a public official announcement on the minutiae of their relationship. But beyond reasonable doubt something going on. Both single, approaching forty. A shared spiritual belief of Christianity and God. A common educational attainment and intelligence. Notwithstanding the appeal of the outdoors, nature, physical activity, cooking, and doing good. More to their friendship than met the eye. Liz had previously committed the cardinal sin. Informing she loved me, during the counselling session—another Christian Counselling Handbook failure.

Rule 1: *Thou will not tell thy clients that thou loveth them.*

Unsurprisingly, unprecedented attention undemonstrative before; a human being engaging, forming attachments and confirming this by hugs and words of affirmation. A strong propensity to fall for it. To have an emotional attachment and connection. All taking place spiritually; ironically. Invisible visual signs or physical manifestations, other than the hugs of course. Occurring in the atmosphere, an unwitting tacit knowledge. Driven by the desire of the soul to be known, loved, and engaged with human life.

The Church Minister had commissioned a charity to operate under the auspices of the Church. A drug rehabilitation programme for recovering addicts. Conceived out of her own son being an addict for many years. Having a presence around Church life, cell groups, counselling, and meetings; a suggestion that I'd be allowed to partake in the project, unacquainted with vices. Every trial, trauma, depression, stress, and psychological tumult faced head-on. Unsupported, acknowledged, or consoled from the incumbents. Experiencing a mutual communal understanding. All broken and damaged. Relationship difficulties, emotional problems, low self-esteem, anxiety, identity issues and a quest of discovering our place in the world. We had followed similar paths with differing terminals. It must have been Grace that saved me. The sentiment and attitude to be righteous; do the right thing. To turn the negative, bitter, angry, stress and anxiety into good works. To forgive, accept, capitulate the pain, loss, grief, disappointment, sadness, and bless others. I couldn't claim credit for these traits but gifted and blessed by God. The quiet voice of reason. Let retribution take her fight elsewhere. Use what the Devil intended for death and channel what God intended for Glory.

As part of the addicts rehabilitation, an outward-bound event had been organised. Three nights camping in Snowdonia, Wales. Hiking up Mt Snowdon, walking and performing domestic duties to engender self-confidence. The invitation extended to me. We were one and the same in terms of our self-worthlessness. But distinct, in that my path was unique. Set apart to be different. Void of swearing, unbecoming. My spoken words were articulate and eloquent, in spite of having uttered few words in many years. The vocabulary had developed unwittingly; not through practised speech but reading, observing, listening, and analysing. Watching the news, referencing the dictionary or thesaurus and the synonyms. Voraciously consuming any artefact of information or data. A penchant for words. My demeanour polite, respectful, well-mannered, and professional.

The second anniversary of counselling looming. Little had changed. 'Kept', afloat, unstable, but static. Static in the emotional tumult, anxiety, stomach pain, chest pain, hysteria, disturbed, obsessively compulsive towards my study, anti-social, and overwhelmed by tormenting spiritual powers. The self-esteem hadn't shifted either, self loathing, shame, guilt, and a sense of being bad still prevailed. The attendees to the trip were Liz, Richard, the guide, six addicts, and me. Liz would drive us there. Borrowing the Pastor's car, an automatic. She would be the self-nominated driver. Her philosophy kicked in that:

"I can do all things through God, achieve and accomplish anything I set my mind to."
"Anything is possible!"
"I can do immeasurably more than I set out!"

We hadn't got beyond the outskirts of Sheffield before we were catapulted back and forth in the car. Thrust to the front with great velocity; launched right back to our resting position a moment later. Jerking, jostled, and jousted. Breaching red traffic lights. An abrupt unexpected and uncertified halt at green. Fellow drivers blasting their horns at immediate emergency stops unannounced. It would play out like this all the way to Snowdon. How someone didn't get thrown through the windscreen was a miracle. How we were able to depart the car unscathed, without trauma, was also beyond belief. You knew you had been on a journey by the time our destination had been reached. For all intents and purposes we could have been navigating the sheep, camel, and cow fraternity of the pothole-ridden sparsely decorated rubble roads of India. But hey, God is good.

The next two days passed uneventfully. Visiting the local town, domestic duties, shopping, cooking, and doing the dishes. The other guys shared two tents, Richard and Liz had their own, and so did I. The time spent was okay; calling in at the local pub before heading back to the camp site to settle down for the night. I hardly spoke. The addicts would dominate the evening with their loud vocals, yelling at each other. Swearing every other word out loud and couldn't construct a meaningful conversation, so I just sat there. It was on the way home. A few of us were walking slightly faster than the others. We must have got fifty yards ahead, not realising how much the gap had widened. A natural human reaction to perform when one senses detachment is to look back. That's what I did. But the revelation would propel me into a frenzy. The sight of Richard and Liz arm in arm; the trigger and ultimate catalyst that did the trick. Spiritually overwhelmed within a split second: knowing. The scenario experienced many times prior. The emotional pain resonating similarly to the bullet ants when Dad repulsed, repelled, and deflected me away from him in the swimming pool during childhood. The chemical shot to the system synonymous to being shot literally. In shock; traumatised. A cloak of despair; excruciating sense of grief fused with rejection, isolation, unconnected and desolate. From this point forward the event concealed and hidden from those nearby. Maintaining my privacy for the point of grieving and feeling the pain alone. They wouldn't understand. The pain was unpalatable and inconceivable. The camp site in complete darkness; lacking public lighting. We'd have to navigate the way through by torch and moonlight. Ironically, benefiting me, as no one could discern my plight. Once in the tent it would climax and release the full venom which it held. Shaking and trembling, irrational, emotionally disturbed, all the self-loathing and self-hate would gravitate to the surface. An epiphany moment. The realisation: what did Liz hold? There must be some emotional attachment for me to resort to this. So, I was right in thinking she had crossed every moral line, broken the Christian Counselling Handbook rules, compromised the counsellor versus counselee relationship. Unbearable; help was required. Nearly twelve midnight. Out of the question to go to Liz's tent and say, I'm freaking cracking up, but you're not the one to love me better. An inconspicuous tool or implement at hand being so far away from home; in a field, in a tent, next to a mountain in the middle of Snowdonia and pitch black dark. The only thing that came to mind was the cutlery used for lunch. Remember seeing the knives in the washing-up bowl. If I could make my way there and back then I'd use the knife. That's what I did. Stumbling over guy-ropes; lost; confused and hysterical. Having acquired what I had gone for, a short dash back in the direction of the tent. Bewildered and disoriented, unsure which was which. Which I had left moments earlier. Unthinkable to enter Richard's and Liz's in this state. After much confusion and recceing each tent. The purpose of intent was achieved. A compulsion to self-harm: not a choice. Didn't actually enjoy doing it. But the spiritual powers and overwhelming emotional concoction equated to a self-destructive action to relieve and console self. By identifying with not only a visual representation but another pain to equal the first pain; made it genuine. The knife was blunt. All there was to do was carve against my wrist multiple times. It didn't cut but wore a deep groove into my skin. Back and forth as though a lumberjack sawing the trunk of a tree. Sawing and gnawing. A sleepless night followed. Troubled and trembling all night long. My tent was practically being blown away as the all-knowing religious lot had positioned the tent in the wrong direction. It became unzipped and the guy ropes loosened; flipping, flapping and appeared to almost take off with the wind. The following morning sombre.

A heaviness surrounded me. Oppressed, unspoken with a descending posture. Broken, traumatised and unresolved. Knew it wasn't good. The scenario hadn't had its conclusion yet. Still more to come. Just a case of time before an identification of symptoms. Whether they would notice my wrist and forehand. Forty-five minutes had elapsed since appearing out of the tent before anyone recognised my state. Liz picked up on it.

"Do you want to go for a walk?" she enquired.

"Yes, I do!" said in desperation.

We didn't go far; just far enough to be away from the group and other campers. A secluded private area near farmers' fields.

"What is it?" she questioned.

Words wouldn't come. An incommensurate amount of grief to interpret into legible translatable codified words. The closer I got to speak the more emotion would rise up. Then all of a sudden it happened.

"I saw Richard and you arm in arm!"

An almighty whaling, howling, uncontrollable and inconsolable sobbing would explode. Up to an hour in duration. Still trembling and shaking, in shock and hyperventilating. Physically, mentally and emotionally exhausting. Rendered floored and incapacitated. The journey home couldn't come fast enough. The allure of my bed to rest and recuperate. It would take days to recover if not weeks. Stupefied and redundant, laid staring in a stupor into oblivion. Negligible duties to perform imminently or pending in terms of college. A relatively quiet week. Perhaps the calm before the storm. The only thing to look forward to was the upcoming next counselling appointment. It was going to be a 'biggie', due to the calamitous ructions in Snowdon. My mind primed and pre-emptive. An extraordinary session. This was wholly significant. Surely, they would have to report it to the Counselling Supervisor; head of the department. Would Liz be reprimanded for her incompetence, breaking and breaching counselling etiquette or steadfast rules? Would she apologise for crossing boundaries, knowingly ignorant of counsellor versus counselee roles and responsibilities? During the interim period the vacant time spent thinking. Reflect and ponder during the week, preceding the session. What had happened and why. Whose fault and where to go from here. Already to discuss, recover, heal, and move on. Liz spoke first:

"How do you think your counselling is going?"
"Okay" I replied, puzzled and confused by the leading questioning.

"Well, just to let you know this will be your last session" she affirmed.

"Based on the events at Snowdon we are no longer going to continue. This will be your last session. How do you feel about that?"

"What the fuck!?"

Incredulous, shocked, amazed, stunned, raging with anger and despair that had not been known previously. My face would depict as much. Bright red with fury. Unable to stifle or quell. The facial expression would have spoken volumes. Without an utterance.

"How do I feel? Are you real?"
Continuing with the current session in vain. They had killed it. Two inept incompetences in one week, not bad.

"I feel like jumping through that window, smashing this room up and launching you two through the window too. Going absolutely full-blown ballistic and smashing my head into the wall. F***ing charlatans!"

"What will you do now?"

"I think I will just go and drive my car as fast as possible into a wall. F*** off!"

Walked out trembling and shaking, confused, disturbed with a vacant destination. A vacuum of sympathy, understanding or emotional intelligence at home. They would abuse some more. Informing to stop the self-pity, moaning, and get over it. Unacknowledged the 'breakdown', regardless, and my social, oral relationship difficulties. Ignorant and clueless but had failed to engage from birth irrespectively.

During the cacophony and mêlée they must have thrown in a comment about having to see a man now. Very convenient. It's the Counselling Supervisor's husband, Phil. Unapologetic, remorseless, and with impunity. Flawless and inculpable. That was it—tough. I would call the supervisor to express my displeasure in this débâcle of counselling. Inform her that abruptly terminating therapy had broken yet another Christian Handbook rule; notwithstanding the moral duty of care to seeking an individual's consent for such a dramatic event. The total absence of communication and dialogue. But beyond reproach. Resolutely stubborn and indifferent; justification for their own failings through my vulnerability.

"But you've got to face men at some point, Jack!"

This wasn't about facing men. A ploy and tactic to absolve and atone for their humongous cock-up. No reasoning with her. They had decided, impressed, predicated and prosecuted upon me.

As we were all attending the same church, inevitable sooner or later our paths would collide. Awkward. They knew what I knew and vice versa. Hostile at best. In spite of the devastation, and void of family or friend to speak to, Liz was the only person I knew to have a conversation or rapport. A natural phenomenon to gravitate towards her. Appearing only feet away from her at the end of the meeting. I must have made reference to some bag she was carrying; a kind of ice-breaker. But she uncharacteristically shrugged it off; failed to make eye contact, rejected me, and walked off dismissive.

CONTINUUM

Within four weeks of seeing Phil he had declared and resolved out of his depth. My set of circumstances were above and beyond what he could offer in terms of therapy. Too complex, deep, protracted and relentless. There wouldn't be a quick fix. I would enquire:

"When will I be well and over it?"
"Will it be months or years?"
"How long does it usually take?"

Having a youthful, naive outlook. Almost a fantasy of one day arriving perfect. I just need to get there. Good on him for having the gumption to admit and confess his limitations and inability to offer a professional service. The outcome of this decision to refer to a specialist professional, a psychotherapist. The letter had been sent to the GP and duly appointed to the waiting list of two years. Within the next two years Phil continuing with regular sessions and offer support at critical times. More of a holding, stabilising scenario or care and maintenance. But again, he and his wife weren't without iniquity either. Randomly absent at agreed appointments. Unapologetic, convinced, and self-justification: would lay the blame on me. My error: I had apparently got it wrong. Beyond reproach and with impunity.

You see, when one has no other living human being in the world to speak to or relate. When one is overtly obsessed, in pain, troubled, anxious, overwhelmed, and heavily burdened by years of horror. With insurmountable stories, experiences, scenes and scenarios to unburden, one will never ever forget or misplace an agreed time and place to do so. When the prime focus from your last departure from doing so, to the next encounter or opportunity to speak, is to premeditate, rehearse, fantasise, dwell, and obsess about what and how you will express in this rare event of opening up and sharing your life. I had never missed an appointment anywhere in my entire life. Not the dentist, doctors, school, interviews, or counselling. Punctuality, the phobia and fear of being late were deeply rooted in my sub-conscious. The irrational, unqualified sense of urgency to avoid the giant that waiting for me if dared to be over the allotted time. Late and absent inconceivable. The paradoxical sense of self, intuition, innate, inherent instinct of knowing that I know would resolve in my head as, "It wasn't me". It was them. Covering their own tracks. Appearing infallible, exploiting my weakness and vulnerability, but also compellingly underestimating my character of being resolute with the truth.

Phil did also refer me to a gentleman at church called Jeremy, to offer some pastoral ministry. The suggestion was that we'd get books out, particularly the Bible, and go through the Psalms on suffering. Jeremy invited me to tea with him and his wife. This was a rare event in itself as I had been uninvited my whole life. The evening emerged as a pleasant surprise. He suggested a walk where we could talk on the way. A very intelligent method of dealing with such an ominous subject. Relaxed, casual, and without intensity or awkwardness. Jeremy had decided to discard the notion that reading the Psalms would somehow offer healing, peace, restoration, sanity, and fix my predicament. It wasn't the Psalms per se: in the context of my needs it wouldn't have made the slightest bit of difference. I had a lot of respect for Jeremy. He seemed the most loving, Godly man I had ever met. Genuinely sincere too. Coming from a perspective of acceptance, listening and befriending. Without the religious talk of what God will or not do; or what you should be praying about and seeking God in. He didn't have the usual glib, flippant, trite quips. He saw I was on a journey and that journey couldn't be halted, modified, or altered in anyway. The beginning, middle, and end were all defined and set in place by God himself. In heaven and on earth. He knows when I sit and rise, my going out, and lying down, familiar in my ways. Such knowledge is too lofty for me to attain.

The journey wasn't tinker-able or fiddle-able. A definite purpose for every episode that had taken place. Called upon at a later date. Similarly to King David, Moses, Job, Joseph, Shadrach, Meshach, and Abednego, Jeremiah, and Saul. God allows circumstances and events to occur because they have greater meaning in the future. Lessons to be learned in these fiery furnaces', wilderness, desolate, and desert barren lands.

As the course was nearing its final semester, mooted talk about the next leg of life. To get a job or to take the academic study another leg up. The word 'Degree' would pop up among the discussions. It had an iconic resonance for me. A codified word that meant so much more. Emblematic or a symbol of ultimate academic achievement. Of stature, respect, intelligence, and authority. This would pacify and fulfil the striving within to be recognised, accepted, and identified. A shining white knight; beacon of glory. For all to see. A somebody. A ratchet up the rank and file of life. A warm positive sensation would permeate my whole body upon hearing this word. Definitely alluring. A far cry from the humble beginnings all too familiar. Unprepared to go back to full-time work. The breakdown still in full flow, another two years to wait for therapy. Studying might be the best route forward. Offering more flexibility and support compared to being employed by a commercial business. Maria and I would research the courses and universities together, most amenable to our circumstances, module choices and level of study. Travelling as a duo and visiting the campus and talking to the course leaders.

Maria would ultimately betray and abandon me at college. Unresponsive or reactionary to what I had committed or not. But through her tinted glasses, the unintended consequence of her troubled and abusive childhood. She had perceived that a male colleague and I had gone for coffee together at the refectory, excluding or failing to invite her. That simple. But unfortunately when you have experienced traumatic events, abandonment, rejection, and forsaken, you look for crises that don't exist. She had sabotaged wilfully an honourable excellent friendship. As much as it hurt and as devastated to lose someone that shared a common understanding, my best friend and ally, understood completely. Sad. She would then buddy up with another male colleague and knowingly skirt by, leaving me behind as though in some retaliation or vindictive retribution and vindication. That makes all things equal and just. A childlike tantrum that would terminate the eighteen months we had shared.

The study of computing and the fascination, the curious, inquisitive allure of technology, software, data, and networks became the idol, crutch, and coping mechanism. Invest my time, thoughts, emotional energy into the paradigm of technology to avoid and escape the tumult within. A safe place. Within this period the Internet was conceived and in its infancy. An exciting opportunity to be able to experiment and explore for the first time how it worked and what we could do with it. It would operate via Modem, dialling a local service provider from your own home and then connecting to the global network of computers. A natural seduction and temptation developed towards chat rooms. Unconcerned who or where. But to engage and communicate: missing threat of abuse or being seen was attractive. It opened a whole new world of social opportunity. Albeit paradoxical. Withdrawn, hidden, isolated but wanting to engage with the world. I could be myself without judgement, criticism, insults, and condemnation. Another escape. A community of my own. Absent of commitments, attachments, roles or responsibilities. Congruous in light of my daily experiences.

22 May 1997 was a wholly significant day in more ways than one. The Labour Party would win the General Election under the leadership of Tony Blair. But more pertinent to me than that was that I had been invited to an interview for a place at

university. In spite of excelling with the grades from Brooks that had been attained in the previous two years. The unforgiving presence of self-doubt, disbelief, lacking in confidence, and low self-esteem would stifle any optimism or hope. Objectively it was a "no brainer". Why wouldn't they accept me? As good a candidate as anyone else with exemplary attendance and attitude to learning. Subjectively, uncertain, fearful, anxious and cautious. A surreal moment when the course leader just dropped it out:

"That's fine!"
Like it was a forgone conclusion. To the point I had to ask for confirmation again.

"Are you sure?" I questioned, puzzled.
"Did you just say, Yes. I'm accepted?"

Unbelievable. Nailed it. Hook, line, and sinker. The course at Brooks would end in June. We would have the summer recess then the university course would commence the second week of September for the new academic semester. I would enrol onto the second year of a four year sandwich course; BSc Software Engineering, as my two years in college were equivalent to the first year of the degree. That wouldn't be easy. All the other students having been acquainted and well established for over a year. Made friends, colleagues, and established groups. I would have to enter as a lone wolf or silent intruder. Without association or connection. On a wing and a prayer. Hoping someone somewhere would find me acceptable to associate. My field-craft days of the Army would come in handy. Along with any SAS or double-agent traits. Lie low, incognito, inconspicuous and undercover. Mingle as though one of them, clandestinely. Appearing as a legitimate, capable authentic student. With every right to be there. Shrugging off any negative thoughts, such as fraud and fantasy.

A temporary employment opportunity had arisen at college for six weeks during the summer holidays. Ostensibly, the governors were entitled to EU funding if they were to incorporate an Intranet into the college information systems. Akin to ticking a box to receive a disproportionate amount of funds, upon satisfying some lofty criterion. It didn't matter to me what the motive was or who was the recipient of the intended funds. What mattered was getting a few quid in the bank for some easy work. Sufficient to buy some tackle, bait, and general fishing paraphernalia for my next jaunt. Also set me in good stead financially for commencing further study missing an income. Therapy had been assigned to a Sheffield Authority therefore remaining in Sheffield. Wisdom to stay at my parents during this period and save on the standard student living costs, accommodation, bills, and food.

The employment position was IT Supervisor. A position of mediocre seniority was surreal. Appealing but incongruous with current self-image. The role to monitor and offer support to the other colleagues that were responsible for data entry, image-manipulation, databases and spreadsheets. Ensuring printers were functioning and sufficient resources of materials. A multitude of people were working on the project. We were all called together on the first morning then accordingly assigned to small groups and delegated to our area of work. Still oppressed, depressed, overwhelmed, and struggling. My senses, intuition, and the instinctive ability to discern, delineate, and discriminate were second to none. I could smell and perceive caustic, abrasive, cold threatening aura from a distance. Tones, audible attitudes, behaviours, words, phrases, and scents would ignite the inherent genetic trait of animal and human alike. To defend and protect oneself. I knew from the outset. The group closest were predatory and should be approached with caution, suspicion, and doubt until otherwise proven innocent. Three of them: all very well acquainted. Had spent the previous two years studying and were essentially all friends together in their own clique. I know from previous personal life experience that wolves prey in packs. Wars are fought and lost with tribes, groups, and communities. A pride of lions, a shoal of fish, a flock of birds. That football teams from the same city war against each other as their own kind are united and attack the opposing opponents to protect and defend their tribe. Similarly, negatively hurting people identify and form allegiances to other like minded damaged, bitter, hurting people. Forming their own unique clique or tribe. Mirroring, affirming and confirming to each other who and what they are, represented as a clan or united solidarity. Justly, collectively bully, attack, contrive surreptitious strategies and plans to undermine. Scapegoating. Belittle and erode a person's ability to defend, protect or sustain themselves. For all intents and purposes they may have worn or shared the same colour of clothing in triplicate as the mindset and persona were identical. Triplets. One and of the same. Extolling virtues of the same unwittingly agreed values. Control, dominate, defend, attack at will pro-actively, exert authority, without weakness or vulnerability. To disparage, curse, insult, criticise, and denigrate any potential threat or unwanted artefact. To unite, and justify each others' actions consistently and diligently.

It wasn't a great start to the six week job, knowing what I knew. Almost wishing otherwise. But suffered many fools in my young years at twenty-five. These wouldn't be the first and no doubt wouldn't be the last either. Seen them off before and would do so again. Despite my broken, weak, vulnerable state. My God-given intuition, artful, skilful ability to identify predators synonymous to my marksmanship principles acquired in the Army during rifle practice. Faced head-on. Failing to perceive from outward appearances, body language, mannerisms or any other external sign or symbol what I was about. Didn't have a brain but a mind. A God-given spirit to slay bears, lions and giants like Goliath. This weak, feeble ailing being would face giants, as David did.

Two of them working a short distance from my group, sharing the same computing peripheral devices. They had an air of superiority, domineering, in control and assuming a position of authority. I'd surmise that my group found me endearing. With my subtle, non-punitive, and pedagogical approach to instruction, training and correction. Softly spoken, gentle, understanding, supportive, and compassionate. But the failing, paper-jammed printer; the focal centrepiece of all the action. Reluctant to meddle, unsure of the problem and fearing it may render worse or inoperable. But so many frustrated students and a backlog in the printer queue, something had to be done. Historically, my sense of root-cause analysis had served me well. Often logical and common sense. But on shutting the printer down a wholly unjustified almighty vitriolic response was launched in my direction. One of the trinity had taken it upon himself to leash an unprovoked attack. Irrational, uncalled for, without cause or reason. Incomprehensible. His face bright red, body language aggressive and warring, a scowl and frown to match. A verbal torrent of obscenities and profanities would follow. Cursing, critical, and insulting. Far and above what the situation called for. Looking at him perplexed, bewildered. What was all the fuss about? We are entering data. Nobody has died, it isn't a life threatening situation. What's up? My reaction or lack thereof must have mirrored how bizarre, unarranted, and ridiculous his emotions had been. Missing the reply but gazed at him, waiting for the next move. But his conviction and conscience must have got the better of him. He slowly receded and lapsed back to normality. My conclusion and interpretation, not to the printer, but his unpredictable outburst, purely motivated by a desire to oppress, exert authority, control, retain power and demonstrate his imaginary role. The printer problem was the conduit, pivot, or catalyst required to justify such an outburst. The cumulative sum of working during leisure time, socially incongruous, agitated, anxious and in the midst of hostility. Enough was enough. Exited the temporary position prematurely without notification. I'm out! Gone fishing.

The looming university start date would expose the proverbial worry. Trepidation, reticence, primed, and the familiar self-doubt. Would I fit in? Would the course be too advanced? Having had such a poor level of basic education. Knowing my Maths was sub standard, this was essentially a science course at a high level. Maths and logic the core syllabus. Incomparable to other students who had taken the traditional route of A-levels, sixth form, or were merely blessed by having a loving mother and father. Supportive, encouraging, creating a solid foundation for a sound functional human being in adulthood. The underdog in every sense of the word. The issue of my adjoining and enrolling onto the second year would also pose as a sticking point. Requiring a huge step of faith, risk, and good fortune that things would proceed as planned. The size of the university was huge in comparison to Brooks. Appearing to be thousands of students. Intimidating and awestruck for the most confident and socially adept of the general English population. A meeting room had been designated for our first reception and to meet our year tutor. Up to one hundred students in this room, primarily male. A shot in the dark or random selection of which row or seat I chose to sit on. Potentially the make or break pivotal moment whether accepted or denied. Depending who sat within reasonable talking distance and whether they would possess the gumption or desire to want to meet someone new. Arrived prematurely early, as was the norm. While waiting for the tutor to introduce himself and take control of proceedings, audible chatter would consume the atmosphere. Returning students from the summer recess who were well acquainted from the previous year's study. I was sat as a lone student. Distinct from all the chatter and social activity. Quiet and solitary in the midst of the frenetic environment. Reminiscent of the induction week at Brooks, when fortuitously Maria and I had sat side by side. A pleasant surprise and amazement that a couple of guys to my left on the same row were being civil. Enquiring who I was and doing there. Informing them of my situation that I'm a squaddie, I mean fresher, newbie student, having graduated from college to commence the second year here. But I don't know anyone or where to go or find my way around. They were immediately sympathetic.

"Don't be on your own, come with us!" they'd say.

This was huge. Instantaneously transformed the immediate outlook to one of hope and positivity. It's going to be okay. Erasing the preconceived notions of being a loner, lost, bewildered, out of my depth, and struggling. They would know the drill and ropes. The etiquette, culture, demands, and expectations. Their one-year former experience invaluable, missing that year. Reassuring, comforting, and welcome. However grateful and blessed, failing to curtail or mitigate what lay beneath, behind, or ahead. The baggage, burdens, yoke of overwhelming weight crushing down. Interfering, disrupting, and enabling chaos to prevail in my day-to-day living. Even though Phil was a backstop or buffer, insufficient for the enduring hours and days where suffering would prevail. Immediate attention was required. In crisis, and it wasn't going away any time soon. It seemed the logical thing to do. To seek out the Student Services Support. Enlist a student counsellor on the campus and grounds of the university. Aligned more closely to my overall student life. Potentially, more gracious and understanding in terms of referring exams or delaying assignments. Extenuating circumstances. Plenty of those to go around. Also cover the interim period while waiting for the psychotherapy appointment. The session two floors below my tutorial and classroom. While in and during the tutorial my mind flooded with distracting thoughts: overwhelming emotion, fighting to stem, suppress and postpone the rage, despair and anger denied. Upon closure of the tutorial, on the hour, I'd have to literally run down the stairs to reach my appointment on time. A fifty-minute slot. Held rigidly. The sooner I could get in, the sooner I could off load and gain some temporary relief, console, redeem: be heard and understood. Sustained sufficiently to allow me to get through another week before the cycle would repeat itself.

The counsellor was a woman, Judy. A singular lone woman. I liked her from the beginning. Now possible for me to identify a genuine, authentic, caring, warm non-aggressive person within minutes. The primal, animal instinct traits, unwittingly and inadvertently acquired through attack, preyed upon, socially outcast, and ostracised. Controlled, manipulated, and coerced to be the weak, feeble runt for ultimate death and destruction. The support on offer would take me right up to the date of commencement of psychotherapy. Her demeanour and aura were gentle and calming. Speaking softly and slowly in a particularly peaceful voice. What I needed. Very appeasing and pacifying. A breath of fresh air. We both knew it was a finite journey, what we would exchange within these four walls. Between her, me, and the tape recorder she would use to have a deeper and more insightful understanding of who I was. Profound. Touching, that someone would have the time or desire to re-listen to me. To really get to know beyond the words but the real essence and interpretation behind them in a deep way. She didn't trivialise or disparage the fact that Dad had failed to send us a birthday card or any personal commendation. She knew the ramifications of that and symbolism. Not the sending of cards per se but the absence of recognition from father to son was huge. She had the intrinsic ability to delineate, discriminate and discern what were conceivably opaque, protracted, and complex issues derived over many years. Unnecessary for me to explicitly state the truth patently, transparently clear. But without stating the obvious, metaphors or synonyms of bygone eras used to convey the current predicament. Holocaust. Apocalypse. Annihilation. Beyond what one is able to suffer. Giants. Numbing of all the constituent parts. Fractured and dissociated. A trinity of mind, emotion, and spirit: mutually exclusive.

Similarly, to college, in spite of the prevailing perennial personal hindrances, the show must go on. The negative energy invested and polarised into the study and research. An avoidance and evasive tactic having a two-fold yield on investment. Dismissing the anxiety, pain, paranoia, burdens, and emotions, while capitalising on the reserve resources to fulfil the goal to achieve. Fellow students or colleagues were unknowing and blind to what was being carried on my shoulders. A yoke of Sin. We were to all intents and purposes, competitors. Competing against each other as though an Olympic event. Defining your role, status, credibility, rank, and file in society.

Jesus said, "*So those that are last now will be first then, and those are first will be last.*" Matthew 20:16

Godless wisdom to think you could be supreme. Engineering your own accolades for self-gratification, pride, and indulgence. God would see that as a fool. Lessons that would only come through correction, chastisement, or humility by God. To be humble, consider others higher than yourself. A servant, not a King. To revere and promote those around you versus promoting self. The current thinking was that of a child. One sin born out of another sin. A counter-response to substandard worth. Indignity and inhumanity.

The following year would present a challenging dilemma: the sandwich year of the course. The student was expected to relocate to an appointed employer to gain industrial experience. The requirement, obliged to travel and live in the designated area for the twelve months. Irrespective how far away from family or friends. Acceptable in principle. But practically nigh on impossible. The psychotherapy still pending, and would present itself around the time I'd be living away. My circumstances dictated that I would need sustained and ongoing support for the foreseeable future. Sending me away to a foreign town, working environment, living and working independently un-conducive to a healthy well-being.

During the interim period, still expected to 'job search', seek out my industrial placement, and ultimately attend interviews with that in mind. The first being at St Albans. It couldn't have been much further away. Another for a government science laboratory in Oxford. A top secret secure location. Many candidates from universities around the country all vying for the same jobs. We'd have to wait at the Oxford train station and be picked up in a transit van, as a group. Reminiscent of Catterick Garrison many years ago when picked up for basic training by the corporals. The group were a majority of male stereotypical geeky types. Reserved, shy, poor social skills. With the exception of one young girl. An extraordinary individual. Eccentric, loud, vitriolic, rude and socially neurotic. Rebelling and breaching all nuances of modern social etiquette. Void of manners and politeness. Bombastic, disrespectful, challenging in-your-face offensive. Caught off guard, as was a standard truism to analyse, observe, discriminate, assess, and conclude. On this occasion an exception. Captivated and bemused by this strange spectacle of unusual display. Akin to a bird's mating ritual of preening, dancing, and flirting. Generally making a song and dance. Allured, charmed, spellbound and beguiling. Suckered in. Unnecessary to compete with other candidates, they were uninterested. The attraction couldn't be explained. Illogical. She wasn't particularly attractive, nor endearing, enamoured with beauty or emanating any love. But a temptation and allure existed, albeit sub-consciously, unwittingly. My mind less focused on the interview and the potential vacancy at hand, but more towards knowing more about Sarah. The return journey back to the station where my immediate attention lay. To repeat and continue the banter, flirting, and amusement. Having departed Oxford for the journey back home, missing the confidence to ask for her number: that was it. But still longing and hoping to resume somehow.

The serendipitous meeting with Sarah had struck a cord of attachment. It often happened that way. The most subtle, inconsequential, meagre attention would render me seduced, transfixed, vying for more. Consumed and pre-occupied with how or when the next enthralling encounter would present itself. A desire and motivation would drive me to seek out, explore, and discover. The little information at hand to go on was her name and university attended. A shot in the dark, but just maybe if I searched on the Internet her name and university domain there could be an email address lurking out there. By great surprise, it unexpectedly appeared instantaneously. An email was quickly cobbled together and sent forthwith. Introducing myself and making reference to the day, time, and place. We would exchange numbers and a possible meeting was tentatively mooted.

An arrangement was made for me to drive down to her parents' house in Leicester where she was currently residing. A strange phenomenon to be in company of another human being. A surreal experience to have uninterrupted one-to-one dialogue. Unfamiliar and out of my comfort zone, unsure and doubting how to behave, conduct and ultimately be. The first meeting, a cosmetic light affair. Talking and drinking coffee. A short trip into town, do the cinema, a bite to eat then leave for home. There wasn't anything conspicuously obvious at this stage in terms of conflict, incongruous, or to suggest we were incompatible or without rapport and connection. Plausible and viable to maintain the connection and call her within the next few weeks. A week had passed and had satisfied an appropriate time to follow up and call her. A difficult confusing call. Appearing a stranger, distant, cold, uncaring, dismissive, responding with one-word replies. Bemused, perplexed, and dejected. I would persevere, grant her grace, accept the current mood, and see beyond it. Dismissing it as odd and she wasn't her self. A few more weeks had passed, and still attempting to make progress, civil, friendly and see where it may lead; by phone. The sentiment and attitude hadn't changed but had become the norm. Abrupt, stoic, abrasive, distant, and without care. For anyone with so much as a mustard seed of self-worth, they'd be out of there short thrift. Viewing patently clear, the wolf in sheep's clothing. A significant threat, ominous and austere. The potential to harm and destroy. But unfortunately, I wasn't one of those that possessed such self-love, care, admiration, respect, and dignity. The silently aggressive nature exhibited would appear normal. Well acquainted, familiar and accustomed. I had learned to relate to it well. On that premise, an invite offered to travel to Oxford, stay overnight and travel to Canterbury the following day for a weekend away with her large group of friends. A student residence building with up to twelve of her acquaintances partaking, unbeknown until arrival.

Prior to the pending date of departure to Oxford, my mood was one of expectant hopeful excitement. Going away to a new city previously unvisited. Meeting new people and having a good leisurely time. Positively optimistic. The drive from Sheffield would take me three hours, missing a break. Exhausted upon arrival. A student house-mate of Sarah's would open the door and greet me. Shouting up the stairs to inform Sarah in her room that she had a guest waiting. Stood there, coat on, bags in hand, waiting. Absent. Minutes went by, left standing and waiting. The house-mates could see how bizarre this was and becoming uncomfortable for all that were in the immediate vicinity. They would shout again.

"Sarah, there's a guy here waiting for you!"
"Send him up!" she replied.

Making my way up the stairs with bags in hands and coat still worn. Entering the room to discover she was laid in bed watching cartoons on the portable TV in front of her. Unresponsive. Transfixed and preoccupied with the events in direct focus. Immutable and intransigent. Unaware of my presence or choosing not to acknowledge the sound of the door opening and a person walking in. Ultimately ignoring me. Eye contact, greeting, and recognition were absent. Stood vacant, bewildered, stupefied at the spectacle before me. It wasn't so shocking as I had been here so many times before. Left bereft. Stunned and shocked unworthy of attention. Ignored, neglected, and rejected. Assumptions and inferences were the only tools available for decisive action. Do I stand, sit, wait, leave? Go downstairs? Tell the other house-mates? I'd remove my coat and put it down at the nearest convenience. Lean or rest my rear end on the closest object. Knowing all the signs, unwelcome. If a drink was required, I'd have to go and make it myself. It wasn't bad enough for me to leave there and then. Hoping this short period would pass, she would stop being difficult and we could resume normal social behaviour.

Her behaviour unchanged; but became standard. The coach journey down to Canterbury awkward. Aloof, critical, judgemental, hard, and cold. It didn't feel good at all. But here we were. Definitely out of my comfort zone. Travelling to an unfamiliar area, with a stranger to meet other like-minded strangers. Didn't bode well at all. She had a very secular worldly behaviour and attitude. Rebellious, revolting, angry, bitter and tormented. Slowly piecing together. Her feet dangling over the seat in front of the cinema. Vehemently opposed to any nuance of etiquette, respectful admiration of rules, standards, and expectations. Sat on the sofa at her parents, she had alluded to the hate for her dad and brother. The venomous tone with which she had spoken. Raging inside that she had been deprived attention through her life. Her dad and brother were so close and he was the shining light, favourite, special one in his dad's eyes. She was essentially superfluous to requirement. Redundant. Missing a father versus daughter relationship. Forsaken for her brother. It became patently apparent what the score was. The aggressive, punitive manifestations would equalise to her damaged, broken, dysfunctional family. Carrying tumultuous burdens of pain, rejection, neglect, and abandonment from her past.

On arrival at the student residence, our final destination, the welcome was luke-warm. All the attention was on Sarah, as it would. Unmentioned who I was or the most brief introduction. An inconvenient bystander. There for the ride. A lap dog. Without social reference and failing introductions, they spoke and conversed with each other. Dis-compassionate and unsympathetic, careless of a lone, shy, vulnerable young man. The agenda for the weekend also unknown. Ostensibly, a day of drinking, day and night. This was turning into my worst nightmare. Didn't tally with my spiritual, righteous, honourable disposition. Didn't agree with antisocial behaviour: negative, destructive effects of alcohol. The social, physical, and emotional harm to self and others, unplanned events that occurred while drunk. I would have to live in the world, but not be of the world. Going along with a caveat of moderating and keeping within my limits. But masquerading to the group that was one of them. Awkward and hostile from the word 'go'. But again, familiar territory. The multitude of occasions the family would speak between themselves, adults to adults, Mum to Dad, acquaintances to acquaintances. Josh to his friends, whereby I wouldn't be allowed to contribute and had to stay shtum or fall victim to the onslaught of verbal and physical abuse. I knew the drill. Well-trodden territory. Hear nothing, see nothing, speak nothing. If asked a question, a mere mutter or utter. Sarah the purported chaperone, had relinquished her role and forsaken me. Void of eye contact, engagement or acknowledgement would prevail. As the day progressed and more pints of alcohol had been sank, the dark spiritual forces would rear their heads. My intuition, self-preservation, and a gift from God would always know my environment. In spite of being tipsy, having too many or full-blown drunk. I knew who was who, location, spiritual atmosphere, motives, and intentions of those present. Sarah would take it to the next level. Not only knowingly ignoring and neglecting, but flirting and chatting up guys in my vicinity. Affectionate, teasing, and seducing kisses. Synonymous to the song and dance she would perform at our student placement interview in Oxford. Parading around, in a flirtatious display coercing attention. The routine and ritual would be repeated. Only this time more dangerous. Copious amounts of alcohol had been downed over many hours. We were theoretically seeing each other. I had been invited as a guest to spend time with her.

The threshold of tolerance gained through the many years, of suffering fools, the uneducated, ignorant, bigots, and damaged people, was exceptional. However, the intelligence was rarely wrong and the threshold had been crossed. Intuition would inform me that what was occurring was an inhumane act. Abuse of social, mental, and emotional proportion, of an individual. The frustration and despair treated this way for so many hours was aggregating and culminating to exploding point. Unbearable. In hindsight the tactic opted probably wasn't the best but in real-time. Don't try this at home. The mitigating circumstances were that I had had too many drinks, was disturbed, irrational, emotional, in pain, perplexed, and confused. But the only method in my arsenal was to kick her up the bum. It wasn't hard. A pacifist after all, and didn't possess a malicious aggressive element in my body. A tap really, to be acknowledged, seen, and identified with.

Absent intuition, message from God, life experience or education could have prepared me for what happened next. An attack of monumental proportion. Similar to a street brawl between two drunken men. It all happened within seconds. In shock at the spectacle that had just taken place. She would pummel me, scrape, and scratch akin to a wild animal. Voracious, vicious, and venomous. Void of dialogue, uncommented, and missing utterance. She walked away and forsook as a casualty, wounded, traumatised, and in pain. Void of further dialogue or conversation that day. Unacknowledged by the fellow drunk group members. As though it had never happened. The flirting, frivolity, rebellious antagonism would continue unabated. Later that evening, decided to go the full hog and end the evening in a nightclub. We would join the long queue and wait our turn for entrance. Still mute since the attack. All of a sudden a voice could be heard from behind. A tone and pitch of shock-horror.

"Mate, mate, look at your neck, what happened... you need to get that seen to! Are you okay?"

My head couldn't take it. Unsure of how to respond. Having had so much negative abuse to hear a sympathetic, compassionate voice was incredulous. Suspicious and unbelieving, shameful, feeling bad, and guilty. Thinking it could just be someone having a laugh and mocking me. Once in the venue I would make a direct route to the toilets and check it out. Sure enough, the guy was right. Huge gashes on the back of my neck, as though I had just wrestled with a bear. Bright red, sore, seeping blood. Obviously, had the location been different, closer to home, within travelling distance, I would have departed long ago. The venue and scene unfamiliar. The coach wouldn't leave until the following morning. Nowhere else to go. It would mean getting through the night and the following morning. To compound things further, I would have to sleep next to Sarah. Knowing her contempt and disdain towards me. She would vehemently resent, despise, and hate me. The following morning continued as the night before. Ignored and unidentified. The time to leave for the coach couldn't come soon enough. Clock-watching and counting the minutes down. Eager and desperate to escape this hell. The mood was emblematic of shell shock. A calm, quiet, dazed, stupefied atmosphere. Silent. Unspoken the whole way back to Oxford. Knowing what each other knew. Without uttering a word. It was obvious I'd never see her again. That no one in their right mind would want to share an environment with a crazed, evil, and disturbed girl. A surreal departure on arrival at the student house. What to say—Thanks for a lovely weekend? Thanks for having me? You were a great host? See you next time? Nothing of the sort. Strolled to the car and looked back. Vacant. Drove the three hours back to Sheffield.

Fortunately, Phil had been a pillar of support, outside the realms of counselling. He had previously invited me to his home and we would have chats in a spare room. An offer was made, that you know where I am if you need me. This was one of those occasions. A crisis. We spoke on the phone and agreed to meet up as soon as. Just to share and offload what had occurred, how traumatic and devastating the experience was and how ill and traumatised I feel. In itself was a great relief. Grateful and satisfied we had resolved between us what, how, and why. Feeling somewhat mitigated but notwithstanding the inevitable fallout. Evidently, consequences and costs for what had occurred. A chat wasn't going to cut it. The following week at home, house bound. Laid on my bed, dazed, mesmerised, and transfixed. Staring into oblivion. Lost, despairing, having no thought or sense. A living corpse for all intents and purposes.

The event would take pole position at the next meeting with Judy. Again, I would present the sequence of events as I did with Phil. Noting the physical violence displayed, several days of social neglect, and mental and verbal abuse. Unreasoned, unjustified, and undeserving. She just listened and absorbed everything I had shared, intently.

"I wonder what the dynamic between you was?
What was the attraction?"

My thought pattern went something like. It's only what I know: familiar, well-trodden ground.

We would agree, a move away un-conducive to my well-being: neither would it facilitate my mental health. The extenuating circumstances and criterion for not complying would be the two years of psychotherapy. An exception. Decided I'd write a letter to the Student Services department to elucidate my point of view and justification for failing to conform. The letter was signed and sealed. 'Private and confidential' emblazoned across the front of the envelope. Handed to the clerk on the front desk, addressed to the manager of the department. Two weeks later passing through the open-plan office. When the clerk yelled across the room to me yards away.

"Hello love! How's the counselling going?"

Dismayed, shocked, and devastated. Suppressing every thought and emotion, not wanting to get thrown off the course at this stage for some ignorant, naive cretin. But silently erupting inside, absolutely incredulous. Stupid f***ing woman. Where do they get these people from?

"You've read it?" I questioned.
"Yes, of course!" she asserted with impunity.

Feeling satisfied, contented, and justified as though she had just scored a goal, with a gleefully proud upright expression on her face. An insidious achievement. Cunningly nasty, with a wry smirk. The Devil would use her to undermine, weaken, disparage, and fulfil his plan for ultimate death. I walked off, indignant, furious, and in disbelief. This would take centre stage at my next appointment. They did eventually grant me permission to stay within Sheffield for the duration of the industrial placement. That resulted in applying to local companies. One of which with an application tendered for was only two miles down the road from my parents' house. A pleasant surprise to discover the hiring manager of the company was Keith, my former tutor at Brooks. He had left that role and moved onto other things. Little did I know now working down the road and the Project Manager. An interview forthcoming. Surmising Keith had recognised my name or not forgotten me. Made a gracious favourable gesture to get me in. Favour—particularly undeserved favour—had been a non-existent feature. To be granted a fortuitous uplift wasn't only unprecedented but immeasurable and imperceptible. Particularly astonishing, given that Keith had no ties to me. Weren't even friends. Owed me nothing. A mere tutor versus student relationship among the multiple other students. One of many. But I had longed for a fatherly, patriarchal, paternal figure for many years. Albeit subconsciously, unwittingly stealth-like. Synonymous to Frank at Warburtons, revering and viewing these strong mature men as substitute or surrogate role models. Keith possessed a natural pastoral, pedagogical demeanour. Between the runt and the God-sent college tutor come project manager; a relationship would ensue. Undefined without covenant. Life, time, and faith would prevail.

There were several other candidates at the interview. It wasn't necessarily a forgone conclusion. A short listing process executed. It did occur I had a head start, an existing connection and mutual understanding. Highly probable the position granted to me as the other applicants appeared mediocre. The call came at home a week later. It was Keith, delighted to be offering the position. We would work together for one year, already acquainted with each other and mutually friendly. To be openly transparent about my predicament, it necessitated informing and explaining my state of affairs. That I had two years of psychotherapy appointments pending. Which would commence two months into the placement. I would have to arrive after 11:30 a m on Tuesday and leave at 3 p.m two weeks later and repeat the cycle. A compromise was made and the decision accepted. The company and Keith would support me in it.

My first year of 'uni', and the last semester approaching closure. Judy was duly informed of the appointed date for commencement of psychotherapy through the local authority. She would indicate our last session looming in the next two weeks. Disappointing yet again to have made an engagement, connection and mutual understanding to be severed and separated. The final session was profound. It would imbue a contrary impression upon my mind and spirit, counter to what had been a truism. She would ask to exchange seats with her. Startled and surprised, almost shocking. A role change. Perplexed, uncomfortable, and realising a paradigm shift from sub-counselee to counsellor. It took several moments to digest and resolve what had just been spoken. Still tentative and unsure, I complied. Curious of what might happen next. She

did accordingly and sat in my seat. We both looked at each other for several moments.
Then she spoke:

"Can you describe to me how you see me?"

Silence. Minutes passed. Then after ruminating, thinking, assimilating, organising, and ordering my reply. Then expressed.

"I find you special, warm, caring, understanding, a listener, intelligent, mature, compassionate, sensitive, gentle, witty, with a sense of humour and very human."

"For you to discern and delineate those traits, you too have those very same traits," she affirmed.

A surreal moment. Monumental...a wholly significant milestone. That would never be forgotten. Finally, I had not only been heard but also seen. How such a trivial experiment could result in such a profound effect upon one's life. A seed had been sown. That only I could recall those precious moments. Informing someone that they are loved, worthy, acceptable, in a convincing way rarely washes. But the art and craft of allowing a person to look into the water and see their own reflection of the beauty: sincere, genuine human they are. An ugly duckling story.

First Love

The chatting online had become a daily mainstay, staple, social, dietary requirement to enter another world, temporarily. Avoid and escape. To console and connect with unknown beings from faraway lands. Foreigners in every sense of the word. Continents away, unrelated, unidentifiable, other than a pseudonym or avatar. A mere gender, age, and country to go on. The chat software in the Nineties was a black screen with real-time typing. The functionality of uploading personal images and sharing your personal life through a time-line would come later in the Internet's development. But here and now a black screen with white text, to someone you had searched randomly across the globe to engage in random trivial conversation. A vent or portal to preserve and hide oneself but also to selectively reveal difficulties, reality of life, and loneliness within. Without overwhelming the opposite of the duo. It didn't matter whether male, female, old, young, Russian, American, African, or Filipino. Any living human being would suffice. A particular one in question was Anne from Florida, USA. We would chat regularly and over time become well acquainted and have some sort of rapport and mutual understanding. She would engage with me in terms of my trials and personal problems. Listen and offer emotional support. The final semester and academic year had terminated and we were now in the summer recess prior to starting the placement with Keith. Desperate to get away. The need of recovery and restoration. A retreat urgently needed. We had joked and mooted the idea of one-day meeting. But the desperate desire, compulsion, and allure to run had reached its apex. What have I got to lose. Unacquainted here. Could go for a week, get a motel near the beach and just chill. There were other people online that I'd chat to too. Investing so many hours over so many months, you got to know a few people. Another in

parallel to Anne was Yasmin. Although that wasn't her avatar or username. Current knowledge that she was from London, female, and twenty-three years old. Again chatting regularly. Hoping to see her online, as we had an instant rapport and mutual connection. Banter, humour, cheeky, flirting, and healthy innocent friendly chat.
A mutual enjoyment, and looked forward to the next encounter. Obvious to both, we were growing and evolving in our virtual friendship. Due to the distance and her personal commitments, we were unspoken on the phone that prematurely. But the clinically depressed state, the Florida jaunt was calling me in. The thought of Miami, beach, and weather. Idyllic and blissful. It's a no-brainer. Let's do it. Within a few weeks I had found the courage and booked it. Having neither met Anne nor having an inkling what she was like in the flesh, a mighty risk. Untravelled abroad on my own. Not to mention so far away as the USA. An event in itself. Whether she would turn up. If we would find each other at the airport. Would we get on or would she abandon me?

The arrival at the airport was fraught. Absent. Panic set in. Lost, bewildered, hot and sweating. Pacing up and down the concourse. All the hellish news stories would come to mind. Turning up a wrong street and being robbed or shot by the local gangs. Appearing a naive, lost tourist trying to find his way, vulnerable and insecure. Paranoia set in. Has she purposely not attended. Did she forget? Was there an accident en route? Missing a phone number or on-going address. I'm done for! Then out of nowhere shouts across the concourse and baggage area. A crazed mad woman, yelling and screaming. Waving arms, gesticulating:

"Jack! Jack! Jack!"

She could be heard throughout the whole airport. Bystanders would think we were long lost brothers and sisters of thirty years, the way she was carrying on. An unsightly spectacle. Now I knew why the portrait photo of her was from the neck up. Obese. Oh well, you win some you lose some. She would drive us back to Ft Lauderdale, Deerfield Beach, where I would stay at my motel. Just relieved to be discovered and collected safely without further tumult. She had to work several days during the week but I was quite happy to be left alone to my own devices. Pondering, reflecting and attempting to make sense of the darkness. Inviting me to her home and her parents. Informing that not everyone is invited here. That I am a rare occasion and special to be spared that privilege. Obviously, there'd be the computer and Internet connection. Available for me to use at my leisure. Astonished when logged in, Yasmin was online. It transpired she was in Nairobi, Kenya, her home town, visiting for a funeral. Again we connected and hit it off. A crescendo building. The mutual desire of wanting to see each other. To put a face to a face. Make it real. We had been chatting several months now and had become close, albeit online. An obvious inevitability that we would soon meet. A tentative agreement was made there and then. When we're both back home. We'll sort out a face-to-face meeting at a half way meeting point. Another risk, uninformed of her physical appearance, other than another head shot she chose to share with me on one of our previous chats. Unsure of her background, social status, mental or emotional state. She had alluded to having just completed an MBA, so that was a good starting point. Including her current place of residence. Kensington, West London. My geography of London wasn't exemplary by any stretch of the imagination, only having visited once when I was sixteen. A coach day trip from Sheffield to Wembley market. But from the terabytes of data that had been consumed over the years from listening and watching the news and documentaries. Educational TV programs, reading newspapers, observing, gleaning and weaning, extrapolating and extricating. Making abstract inferences on the world about me. I knew of Kensington Palace. West London was registered in my mind as the better part of London. The 'well-to-do' area. Where foreign embassies reside: dignitaries wine, dine, and spend their lavish lifestyles. Wealthy foreigners, Russian oligarchs, film stars, musicians, and celebrities buy up extortionately priced property.

The short break with Anne would serve its purpose. A brief retreat, sanctuary, rest, escape, and the hope of solace. Under no illusion that that's all it was. The root cause and underlying iniquities would still need to be addressed. This had served as a resting place. But the intrepid journey far from over. On arrival back home, business as usual. With the exception of the pending meeting with Yasmin coming. Something to look forward to. Missing an official 'girlfriend' as yet. Only brief encounters of being screwed around, abused, and emotionally played with. An incredible self-doubt, insecurity, ignorance: uninformed, lacking in education about personal relationships. How to treat women, etiquette, and girlfriend versus boyfriend nuances.

The Mars and Venus book had been read, hoping to glean some insightful tips and 'how to's' in the realm of the dating game. But not really knowing how or when one should act or behave. Lost in another terrain, out of my depth. Would she catch on that I was emotionally defunct, void of feeling, missing personality, and mummified? Could I mask it, appear normal, and offer some pretence? But it wasn't me. Never any good at lying or concealing untruths. My inner moral code and righteous gifting from God would see me as transparent, genuine, and authentic as they come. Will not mimic, portray, or present anything other than the real me. Flawed failing underdog—take me as I am.

The pending psychotherapy was an overarching concern. In the thick of it, trying to concentrate on developing database and management information systems: it was always hanging over me. Counting the days down to my first appointment. Would it be a man or woman? What would they be like? What would be encountered during these sessions and the many that would follow in the coming two years? Would it finish me off? Would I still be able to maintain my position as a student on the placement with Keith, or forced to forsake it? Even if I managed this year, what would the final year of uni be like? Would I have to relinquish my studies and quit?

Birmingham was elected the inaugural meeting destination. Approximately halfway between London and Sheffield. We'd each get the train and meet at the central station. Immeasurably exciting. A virtual connection with someone and then to be bringing it into the physical realm. Back to reality. A genuine human being who wants to know me, converse, and relate. A reciprocal arrangement.

A paranormal phenomenon in the world of Jack. Hindered and impeded; socially inept. Deficient in self-confidence and self-worth. Potentially a tall order to carry it off. Nervous and anxious as was the norm.

We hit it off straight away. Like we'd been friends for years and this was a reunion. I liked her from the off. Well-spoken, lovely voice, charming, oozing with personality and exuberant with it too. A real lady. My fantasy had always been one of old-fashioned courtship. Whereby the man plays his gentlemanly role and the woman takes on the lady-like role. He serves her and meets her every need, adoring and accommodating her wants and desires. The idea of opening doors, allowing the lady to walk through the doors first, had been in my mindset since childhood. A far cry from the modern contemporary dating and relationship scene. Whereby a mutual desperation takes place, rushes in, forces and fabricates something flawed. To engage in a shallow, superficial arrangement based primarily on the physical element. It was dignified, respectful, patient, and kind. Loving. We wouldn't stay long as it was the first meeting. A chance to see each other physically and confirm that we relate and have a rapport in the real world. We'd step out into town, have a coffee nearby, then go on to have lunch within another short walk. Before returning back to the station for our respective journeys' back home. Internally, like a giddy kid.

Excitable. The atmosphere had nailed it for me. Obvious. The connection, rapport, banter, cheeky flirting, and good conversation. Far beyond expectation. A calling to the toilet would temporarily take me away from the table. Giving some quiet thoughtful reflection and contemplation how the last two hours had gone. Unbelievable. Absolutely unbelievable. The giddiness proving difficult to suppress. The return trip back to the table would see me with a big cheeky-boy wry smile emblazoned across my face.

"What's up with you?" she asked.
"Nothing!" I replied.

Grin extending its original position. The face lit up with abundant joy. Enjoyable beyond words. Feelings unfamiliar or sensed ever before. A warm glow from within would confirm the thoughts of happiness. On my return to the table, passed the bar and paid the bill. Having meagre funds and living a student life on grants and loans, money was tight. It had broke me getting the train journey down to Birmingham. But these were my principles. That a man would serve, chaperone, and minister to his partner. Once lunch was over and had time to settle. We would make a move. On departing the restaurant she would stop at the bar, suggestive of waiting to pay the bill.

"What are you doing?" I questioned.
"Paying the bill" she replied.
"It's okay, I've got it covered. I already paid."

Obvious and evident she was used to paying for everything. But important to me despite being skint and having a financially poor existence. She wouldn't know what I had or could afford. Our fun and frolics would continue right up to the platform edge at the train station. Evidently, neither person wanted to part. We would have liked the day to continue. Absent expectations. Only grateful of the time we had spent, hopeful and optimistic of a continuation and the next encounter. Similar, to a scene from a movie. The ultimate departure. Synonymous to the Vera Lynn song, We'll Meet Again. The train waiting at the platform. A loving couple about to say their goodbyes. Heart's torn apart. As the aforementioned alluded to, no handbook had been read about when one meets a new girl, how to leave it. Unsure whether to shake her hand, walk off, or just stand vacant while she turned to get on the train. Inhibitions were amplified in public. Conscious of what people think. Paradoxically, a fear of being seen, in spite of unseen. Being watched made me anxious and uncomfortable. But unaware how it came about we would embrace and kiss. Never having really had a proper kiss prior. This was like rocket fuel. Especially with someone I so admired, liked, and wanted to be with. Aware of the other by-standers waiting for their train. Staring at the spectacle before them. Kissing and expressing loving affection in a public area. My eyes would wander and be perturbed by the looks and stares. But people are looking at us, we should stop right now, came the thought. Then the next thought. Don't you dare stop right now. You will absolutely never forgive yourself. Keep going. That was it. A fantastic time and an unforgettable parting, to be hopefully resumed soon.

Sealed with a kiss, literally. A trial to contain myself on the way home. Inexperienced emotions of life, energy, excitement, hope, joy, and happiness. I wondered if I kissed her the right way? What she thought of it? This would play with my mind for the duration. Will she be in touch? How soon?

An hour into the train journey, a text message appeared on my phone. It read, "Thank you for an amazing time! Can't wait to see you again soon."

Now confirmed in writing. This is surreal. Is this really happening? I need to wake up from this dream. The coming days we'd be talking on the phone for hours. Sometimes up to three hours without a break. Occasionally unspoken but just being with each other at distance. Offering me a bite to eat of the sandwich she was eating, sharing the music in the background listened to. The friendship became intense, texting, calling, thinking about each other in our absence. We couldn't wait for the next meeting. Her personal schedule would delay any imminent arrangement but within another two weeks we had set another date: Leicester.

Leicester was a similar distance to Birmingham. A half way meeting point. We'd meet for the day, returning home in the evening. A beautiful summer's day. Early May. Blue skies, bright sunshine and warm. A day to be outdoors. We'd find each other and meander to the nearest park. A whole park to ourselves. Sat on the grass feeding each other cherries, spending quality-time slowly getting to know each other a little deeper. My confession was one of openness and transparency. Uninhibited in terms of revealing my past and origin. From a working-class family, dysfunctional at that. In the midst of a breakdown and suffering depression. She was unphased, irrelevant. Liked and accepted just as I was. Alluding to her privileged education in Switzerland and the four languages she spoke. Muslim, Asian ethnicity and originating from Nairobi, Kenya. Highly educated, having just completed an MBA. A descendent of great wealth and a global empire. We were worlds apart but symbiotic. Intrinsically connected, natural, and effortless. Congruent. The experience was blissful. Unfamiliar, alien, and bizarre at the same time. Long periods of uninterrupted pleasure and personal enjoyment. Carefree, unrestricted in a bubble of love. The only minor interruptions my clock-watching. Fearing the imminent departure when the day would finally close. Not wanting it to end. A sense that was shared mutually. Frustrated that this happy time could not prevail for a little longer. It was on the short stroll back to the station, the sunset and dusk setting in soon after. A gorgeous evening. A shame to terminate it there and then. But I arrived unprepared only in the three-quarter length pants I had and a t-shirt: summery clothes.

"Shall we get a hotel?", popping out of the blue, she queried.
"What?"
"You know, shall we stay over?"
"But how, when, where? We don't have any luggage or toiletries!"
"That doesn't matter! It'll be fun. Let's do it!"

She was that kind of person, carefree, extremist, risk-taker. In contrast to my rigid, fixed moral code. A breath of fresh air to be so spontaneous, speculative, and make a spur-of-the-moment decision. The evening full of excitement. Like two young kids truanting. Giddy, liberated, and riding the wave of ultimate freedom. Breaking the rules and norms of normal social etiquette. We'd call a local pizza takeaway company and have dinner delivered. The word 'Dinner' was a learning experience per se. For us northerners, 'dinner' was 'lunch' and the meal in the evening was 'tea'. The subtle differences in our cultures, social status, and class apparent. Symbolising our disparity although a congruent one. Sitting on the bed, eating pizza, followed by chocolate fudge cake. Talking, sharing stories and life experiences. Getting to know each other more intimately, step by step. On one level quite conceivable to think, way out of my depth. Akin to meeting royalty or some aristocratic princess, or a scene from the Victorian era when servants and those of the lowest ranks were not allowed to frequent or relate to the higher classes. But on another level so fitting. Hand in glove. Peas in pod. Made to measure and snug. Heaven-like. A dream come true. An unprecedented occasion in my life for such a treat to be experienced. To spend unlimited funds without concern or worry to pleasure oneself and enjoy. Able to share those precious moments with such a wonderful person was in addition and a double blessing. A time to pinch oneself and wake up from the dream. Missing a young girlfriend ever before, not to mention about to spend the night for the first time, out of my comfort zone yet again. Unsure of what or how to be. When to strike or not to strike. But sense of self and the desire to do the right honourable gesture, the intuition and gut feeling expressed that beyond grateful for the present. The role of the gentlemanly facet would respect and honour her. What we had, so much more than sex. The following morning we'd check out, make our way back to the train station and on to our respective journeys' back home. The coming days a repeat of the recent past. Calling, texting, thinking of each other. Unable to wait for the next encounter. How long till I see you again?, we would both say. She mentioned that her friend had a grandmother in Manchester, whom she was keen to visit. Suggested they go together, hiring a car from London, picking me up along the way and I drive them to Manchester. Leave her friend with her grandmother and we spend the weekend together. Before making the same return journey back home. Manchester it was, in another two weeks.

As planned and expected they would arrive at my parents' house in the hire car. Alex, her friend, was stunningly beautiful, attractive, young, and voluptuous. They had met at boarding school and were childhood friends that lasted to the present moment. Alex was born in England, but lived in Guadalajara, Mexico. Once meeting me, Yasmin was keen to affirm to her that I was what she said.

"Can you see it?" Yasmin enquired.
"Yes, you're right. There's definitely something special about him," responded Alex.

It didn't get much better. Two beautiful women in the car, driving a sporty VW Golf TDI across the Pennines towards Manchester to spend my first weekend away with my best new friend. Yasmin beside me, holding my hand as I rested it on the gear stick at a standstill. The responsibility of booking the hotel had been bequeathed to me. Though she had done this hundreds of times before. She felt I should do it. Having never booked a room before, anxiety set in. Our expectations were likely to differ in terms of standards and cost. My budget limited. But then, wouldn't want to kill the momentum by ending up in low-end, substandard, uninhabitable lodgings. Leaving her unimpressed. Ill equipped to impress irrespectively. A decision would have to be made to go down the middle. An average mid-low-end price. The worry and anxiety would consume me. Thinking of failure. Disappointment of the shoddy, ageing, substandard decor. Judging me on first performance of acting in a gentlemanly role. Obviously incomparable to her standards of several hundred pounds per night. But it was what it was. In hindsight it served as the perfect antidote and best outcome. Testing me. To determine if shallow, would go to great extravagance to buy her charms, or if modest, humble and unafraid to reveal sensitivity or weakness. A paradoxical outcome. My vulnerability, openness, genuine sincerity, and honesty won the day. Unafraid to laugh at oneself or make fun of failings. The room average, as expected. Acceptable for what it was. The only impediment, the sloping floor.

She had expressed on several occasions in recent weeks she loved me. Love before had been and was a dirty word. Not even a word. Unheard or uttered. From parents, relatives absent, only in body. It struck me strange and obscure. An inability to interpret or translate and then process. Taken aback: perplexed. Unsure of how to respond. Thank you! You're welcome!, or pure silence? This would take some resolving; can't deal with it. The first reaction to dismiss, deny, and forsake. Take it as compliment or possible platitude. It would probably blow over and be a mere transient, temporal term of endearment. Constant reminders and affirmations of, "I love you!". Even missing confirmation or my reciprocal response. It was obvious my walls, self-preservation and protectionism, had guarded entry. But the dilemma would present itself. Will you allow her in to Love you or keep her out and fail to experience a journey of love. Dare to connect. A once-in-a-lifetime opportunity to love and be loved, 'to be in love'. The next few weeks spent wrestling and deliberating thoughts, insecurities, threats and opportunities. How long could I go on like this, indecisive? I wanted it. I chose love. By my will, to allow her in and receive what she may give to me and vice versa. I would love her.

The weekend stymied by an unfortunate realisation. Yasmin's traditional annual family holiday pending: the Caribbean on a six-week cruise. Un-allowed to abstain or opt out, everyone should attend. The family's tradition, missing excuse. It meant we would not see each other for that period. Also, her views on the Muslim faith suggested we didn't have any real future. A blip: a short-term affair. She had aspirations for a global career in the USA. Ultimately, would have to enter an arranged marriage, as set out by her religion, community, and family. Nigh on impossible that we were ever going to settle down and spend the rest of our lives together. Gutted, dejected, demoralised and sad. Unwittingly, I had fallen in love with her. Feelings were now in play. Sharing an attachment and emotional connection. We were in love. Acknowledging my disappointment, she had written a card for me. She often sent me cards. Just to say, I love you. Thinking of you and can't wait to see you again soon. On occasion, just a cute baby's face, noting, 'When I saw this I thought of you.' Explaining that the present moment shouldn't be forsaken. Better to have loved and lost than to have never loved at all. Which was my paraphrased version. My view was to end it now to prevent further hurt, loss, grief, and disappointment. But her contrary view of making the best of the moment; cherishing precious times to be remembered forever was the best course of action. I didn't necessarily agree but could understand an opposing opinion. Defensively, my primal man would want to resist the detachment and separation. Manifested through offers of studying in the USA to be near her, converting to the Muslim faith, or any esoteric option to be united. Our time together was finite. An ultimate ending in the near future. Unwilling to spoil the present, the topic put to bed until nearer the time. We would continue uninterrupted and unhindered.

The psychotherapy appointment had stealthily crept up in the midst of the captivating, surreal life changing few months with Yasmin. Looking forward to what lay ahead, a desire to face issues, gain insight, resolve, and move on. But eyes wide open to the reality; conceivably overwhelmingly devastating. Rendered defunct, incapacitated and cabbage-like. Unquantifiable. A journey in its own right. A tributary, subservient to the ultimate journey. The building iconic within the psychology field. Befitting and grandiose, built c.1855, a Grade II listed building. White and clinical. Overbearing and synonymous with the contemporary institutions of former generations colloquially known as asylums.

Once signed in at reception, the waiting room lay a few short steps away. Waiting patiently for your therapist to collect, on the given time, precisely. Several other patients or misfits also in attendance. Having arrived at the same place through similar journeys. Manifesting anxiety, personality, and obsessive disorders. Incongruous with self and tormented souls. The assigned therapist a woman called Helena. First impressions were of calm, quiet, peaceful, and academic. Impressions were all you had to go on. An omission of small talk, introductions, personal enquiries, or terms of endearment. From your name being called to arrival at the designated room, shtum. Leading the way, and I would follow. Observing her shoes, delicate tentative steps, clothing, posture, and body language. To glean and wean to discern any iota of evidence that would grant me knowledge and insight to her. She would almost glide up the stairs, so gracious and effortless. Exuding peace, tranquillity, and humanity at its best. Enchanting. A spectacle per se. Her flat shoes interpreted as someone of middle class, a librarian studious and academic type. Plain, basic, and simple. Unobtrusive. She wore all black. Making a character-judgement unattainable. Negligible evidence to go on. Would have to accept as was. This time unknowing who or what I was relating to or sharing my greatest fears, shame, pain, loss, grief, heart, vulnerabilities, and ultimate self. Usually, if aware of how potentially threatening the adversary was, my defences, behaviour, speech and body language would act accordingly. But void of intelligence, information and leads to go on, nigh on impossible. A blank slate or white board. She had made an impression already before we had begun. Immediately an honorary reverent respect was bestowed upon her. Without cause or reason. Merely out of our spirits colliding.

The room another iconic emblematic setting of the shrink's office, or the psychologists therapy room. A small four metre^2 room, a desk, chair, and the proverbial shrink's couch. On entering, silent. She sat in the chair and I assumed the position and dutifully sat on the couch upright. We were at 90° to each other. Missing an advisory, induction, or guidelines on therapy etiquette, but got the distinct feeling we shouldn't be having eye contact. It wasn't that kind of setup. She presented a subtle mild intimation and innocuous suggestion that the couch was there to lay down upon.

Void of personal dialogue or discourse. My own research had revealed the concept as 'transference'. One speaks, another reciprocates, and out of the two interactions a third phenomenon appears, which is insight or epiphany. Still absent dialogue. My mind working over time. Should I be sat this way, arms folded, guarded and defensively? At which point will she say something? Is this a waiting game? The clock on the wall let me know five minutes had elapsed and that was wasted time. I've got fifty five-left. Is she going to get her skates on? I can't sit or be anyway. This is what I know. Immutable. If she doesn't like it she's going to have to lump it because I can't move. The frustration building. She would look directly ahead: my sight was directed straight ahead from my posture, across to the window. Our line of sight would intercept and cross the juncture in the middle of the room but our eyes would not meet.

Ructions were erupting and quarrelling within my spirit. Uncomfortable and agitated. My conditioning and familiar behaviour of respect, righteousness, polite and well-mannered, would see me un-interrupt proceedings or offend. Warring interior factions would remonstrate, contend, and conflict with each other. The conscious common sense approach to, "Are you going to say something then?", to reserved, introverted over the top polite, people-pleasing, fearful childlike insecurities. This crescendo would soon reach its pinnacle and ultimate climax. Despairing and frustrated by the wasted minutes. A perennial stickler for productivity, efficiency, and making the most of every given moment. It went against my moral code to be inefficient, redundant, and in vain.

The dam wall would then begin to weaken, crack, and subside.

"Are you going to say something then?" I said, with a frustrated impatient tone.
Moments elapsed before a reply was forthcoming.

"I wonder why you think I should instigate or lead the initial conversation," she replied.

That was it. An open-ended exclamation of sorts. Leaving an unanswered query at my liberty. A question of monolithic proportion. Conceivably, that question could encompass my whole life from beginning to end in one sentence. It had so much in it, but so succinct. Striking, shocking, and bewildering at the same time. The memories of a bygone era would come flooding back. The time Josh would raise is hand on my behalf and ask the teacher if I could go to the toilet. That he was the more forward, social, and confident. Contrary to my low self-esteem, inadequacy: shy and withdrawn. Experiencing the old saying of 'Children are seen but not heard', adults, family, and relatives relating and conversing between themselves, missing attention. Neglected at home, school, and in the street. An epiphany would light up my mind. Got it, that's why. The thinking being, rude to speak first, you speak when spoken to. Josh had always led and I followed. Dad failing to acknowledge, nor give me eye contact. Mother would leave me to go and attend some more pleasurable pastime. Even on the rare occasion a word was uttered, I'd be shot down in verbal abuse short thrift. Silencing, quelling, oppressing, and socially drowning the person within. Unthinkable and incapacitated to instigate a conversation. Fear, conditioning, and familiar behaviour demonstrated in early childhood. Bound in bondage. Spiritually and mentally locked up as prosecuted by my immediate environment.

We had broken the ice and the conversation had begun. A starting point from which to build upon.

The first few weeks working with Keith at the student placement passed uneventful. Taking solace and comfort in that it was local, Keith familiar, known, and would watch over me more so than a foreign co-worker, stranger. Although he did say:

"The best thing you can do now is go around all the offices and make yourself known. Introduce yourself to potential working colleagues."

The metaphorical alarm bells and sirens would ring and wail in my head. Alert, panic, evacuate, seek out the escape route. Inconceivable to think I could just walk up to a complete stranger and say, "Hello, I'm Jack!" The fear of rejection, dislike, dismissal, fobbing off, burdensome, and an inconvenience were all too great. The walls of self-preservation, protection, and sustainability would render me paralysed. A paralysis of mind, spirit, and emotion. Departing my desk en route to the toilet, hovering in the kitchen, walking around the office and appropriately appearing back at my desk. The open-plan office scanned, recce executed, recorded intelligence received, and acted upon accordingly. They look busy: don't want to be interrupted. What would I say after that? I'll go bright red: look and feel ashamed, awkward, agitated, and wishing I'd never approached them. I'll just leave it.

Yasmin and I would continue our 'Love Affair'. Spontaneously and randomly meeting and spending weekends wherever the moment took us. A far cry from my humble beginnings. An epic storyline by any stretch of the imagination. From orphaned runt born into poverty, idolised, worshipped, loved, and living on the crest of a wave. Frequenting restaurants unforeseen, fine dining, and plush-plosh hotels. Served and waited. Taxis, hire cars, gifts, presents, and undeserved treats. My wish at her command. She would invariably order the drinks or food for us both. Knowing full well, the male role to perform that duty. Serve his beloved and wait on her. But in reality my self-confidence or lack thereof—zero. The key indicator: unable to speak to the waiting staff and order our chosen items. Withdrawing and retreating into self. Doubting, intimidated, fearing, unacquainted with the grandeur atmosphere and professionalism in the restaurant environment. Out of my depth, socially, culturally, and by class. She lived this life perennially. A normal everyday occurrence: second home. Naturally and comfortably assertive and self-confident in public spaces. Another notable act on leaving the restaurant: she would yell, hail, and wail at a taxi. Frenetically gesticulating, waving arms in the air, as though Robinson Crusoe on a desert island, waving to a boat in the distance. Something that would render me taken aback. Mesmerised at this improvised and spontaneous act of free uninhibited expression. Failing to have witnessed or experienced such life, zeal, and vigour emanate from a person before. It had highlighted my dysfunction or disability. Exposed flaws, weakness, and vulnerability. An eye-opener. That you can be so confident and outwardly expressive in public and use it to your advantage. I want some of that.

We would elope to Cambridge, Oxford, Leicester, and London itself. A blissful idyllic ideal. But wittingly finite. The intuition and inner sense of self knew it was the real-deal. This is what they mean when they talk about falling in love. Hook, line, and sinker. I'd got it. Whatever would happen from here on out, at least I could say I had experienced real, genuine, authentic love. From such a regal, revered, admirable, and desirable person at that. She had men throwing themselves at her daily. Able to take her pick, receiving multiple advances on an average night out. A myriad of potential candidates were at her whim and disposal. Across the globe. High-flyers, CEO's, entrepreneurs, princes, Asian, European, American, Indian, and London. But no ... Fell for an orphaned runt from a dystopian melancholic community based in Yorkshire. Poorly educated, socially inept, deprived, broken, and lost.

The following therapy appointments with Helena exposed my worst fears. Overwhelmingly difficult. Physically, mentally, emotionally, and spiritually. It would render defunct, cabbage-like, and incapacitated. Feeling overburdened, a heavy weight pressing down from above. Deeply depressed, poor mental capacity, numb and void.

The one-hour floor was mine to do with it how I saw fit. The topics, issues, starting and finishing points were all at my behest. Would unpack and lay out my day-to-day living experiences. Void of a single person in the world to confide in or share my desperation. Ill at ease with self. A tormented soul. Chuntering and chattering in my head, from my shoulder. The parrot that would perch there daily at its choosing. A euphemism for the Devil incarnate. Audibly critical, condescending, berating, callous, disparaging, and derogatory. Punishing and persecuting. An enemy within. Negative curses of an evil nature.

"What are you doing it like that for?"

"You don't do it like that, stupid!"
"You'll never make it, idiot!"
"You're doing it wrong again, loser!"
"It's not good enough, you'll have to do better."
"Don't dare speak, or I'll have you!"

Leaving the building, a shed load of extra insight, previous unknowns, and epiphanies would have been interjected into my consciousness. Perplexed, confused, and dazed. Then a reality check. The optimum most desirable imminent objective to go home to bed and sleep it off. Sit and allow my mind to interpret what had been discovered. But in reality, the student placement with Keith was calling me. A journey across town to the company's location, to start work as though uneventful. Repeating this behaviour for the duration of therapy. Also, leaving work on Thursday at 2:30 p.m, to drive across town and start exploring and discovering who I was.

EPILOGUE

This isn't the end but only the beginning. The story has only just begun. The continuation and subsequent scenes, events, and relationship developments will be presented and portrayed in God, The Devil And I, Volume Two.

Will the love affair with Yasmin continue or terminate? Would therapy with Helena become too much and end prematurely? Or would working with Keith be so overwhelming I'd have to relinquish my duties? Surmountable to graduate the degree?

GLOSSARY

A-Levels	Highest level of the standard level of education
CV	Curriculum Vitae otherwise known as a Resume within North America
Butlins	A popular well known holiday camp
Bed-wetters	Children that urinate in their sleep
Cell Group	A small group of believers that meet regularly to discuss the Bible
Copper	English slang for a policeman
Dole	English slang for being unemployed
Gateway	A nationally renowned local supermarket chain
Kwikfit	A tyre company in England renowned for changing tyres quickly
GP	General Practitioner (local Doctor)
M1	The major motorway artery through England
mph	Abbreviation – miles per hour
Outdoorsy	A love of open spaces, countryside and outdoors
Pub	Public House (To consume alcohol legally in a communal building)
P.E	Physical Education
Peg	A specific fishing place on a pond or river
Pontins:	A popular well known holiday camp
Quid	Slang for one pound sterling cash

Recce	Reconnaissance (analysis and assessment of the situation)
Snap	English slang for pack-lunch, food during break-times at work
Snog	English slang for an extended kiss
Suffragettes	In this context is contrived as suffering individuals
Telly	Television
Tots	A colloquial term meaning small children

This page is intentionally left blank.

Printed by CreateSpace.

First Printing, 2014

info@god-thedevil-andi.com

ISBN: 978-0-9930452-3-3

Printed in Dunstable, United Kingdom

91222385R00118